ANGELS WITH FUR

Inspirational Stories For Animal Lovers

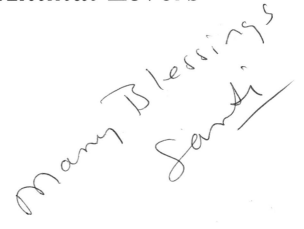

Many Blessings
Santi

Pamela Santi Meunier, M.A.

Galactica Press

ISBN 0-9669095-I-8
Cover Design by Patrick J. Falso
Photographs by Adam Mastoon
Printed in the United States of America

This book is dedicated to all of God's Heavenly creatures
who humbly come to the earth to serve and teach
humankind the true qualities of loyalty, steadfastness,
whimsy, joy and most importantly, unconditional love.

With a heart filled with gratitude, I dedicate this book to
those tireless companions of comfort and great strength,

God's angels with fur.

Acknowledgements

I want to thank the wonderful writers that contributed their heart-warming animal stories for this book. It would not have been possible without your generosity.

Cassia Berman
Joan Embree
Susan Jones
Kate Kennedy
Marty Klein
Mia LeComte
Sarah Manuel
A.M.N.
Kate Solisti

I also want to thank the wonderful poets and philosophers for their words of wisdom and insight.

Special thanks for all your hard work and skill:
Karen Miller, Susan Happ, and Kris Lima

Contents

Foreword

by Michael Learned

"Ma" of *The Waltons*

My young niece Sash, when asked at school what comprised the universe, replied, "many mysteries". A perfect answer as far as I'm concerned.

This lovely book reveals the mysterious relationship and wondrous love that animals and humans can share with each other: the ability to communicate without words; the amazing courage and generosity our animal friends have taught us; and their willingness to serve and forgive us over and over as we stumble through life.

My husband informed me, when we were courting, that he hated cats. Of course whenever we visited friends with felines, the first person the furry ones would head for would be my sweetheart. His response was always, "You're barkin' up the wrong tree, pal!"

When I was performing in "Sisters Rosensweig" in New York, a young actress found a tiny black kitten wandering in an alley. She took it home only to discover that her two cats, already in residence, had no intention of sharing living space with this tiny interloper. She brought it back to the theater and in a moment of loving madness, I said, "I'll take it!" Home we went to my apartment, where Miss Kitty played and delighted. I fell instantly in love. But how to tell John, who was living in L.A. and not only hated cats, but generally thought of animals as much lesser beings than humans?

A week later when I broke the news, he hit the roof. He was due in New York for the weekend and elicited a promise that the cat would not sleep with us or, indeed, even sleep in the same room. I didn't like him very much at that moment, but agreed nonetheless. John didn't waver. Even my feeble attempts to assure him that kittens and cats were not the same met with stony silence. He was unmoved when he saw the little ball of fuzz on the living room couch and didn't find Miss Kitty's antics cute or amusing.

Our first night together after a month of being apart started with John reading a book, me tossing and turning, and Miss Kitty howling piteously on the other side of the bedroom door. After about an hour, I told my husband he was a heartless brute and that I intended to sleep with Miss Kitty on the livingroom couch. The heartless brute capitulated and Miss Kitty, tail in the air, wobbled her way into our boudoir and climbed expertly onto our bed. The following morning when John awoke to find a warm little doughnut purring on his chest, he was gone. Their ensuing love affair was a mighty one and when some thoughtless speeding driver took Miss Kitty away from us, I saw my husband weep for the first time. We miss her to this day, and she is the only other woman (female?) he ever sang to.

For those of you who love animals as I do, this book will make you laugh and cry. For those of you who aren't familiar with the joys, sorrows, and learning experiences connected with animals, this book will open your eyes and hearts. You will swim with the dolphins, talk to a horse, roam with a hound dog, and explore "the mysteries".

❁❁❁❁❁❁❁

Michael Learned, an actress, lives with her husband, John Doherty, in Los Angeles. They share their hearts with Jolo, a cat, and Poloma, a delightful and demanding Boston Bull Terrier.

Chapter One

"He thought he kept the universe alone;
For all the voice in answer he could wake
Was but the mocking echo of his own."
- Robert Frost

Our Friends Indeed

"Love Lifts Us Up Where We Belong"
- Joe Cocker

Animals Rescue

Recently the news was filled with what everyone viewed as a truly amazing event: an eight-year-old female gorilla named Binti saved a small boy who had fallen some eighteen feet into her habitat. Binti, a mother herself, kept the other gorillas away from the child as she gently picked him up and carried him to the zoo keeper's door. The crowd of onlooker's watched in amazement. Although Binti had been raised by humans, this alone may not fully explain her caring behavior. Several years ago in an English zoo, a male gorilla who was neither raised by humans nor possessed Binti's maternal instincts did much the same thing when a child fell into his habitat. He did, however, take the child to safety. Why?

The newspaper *Trust of India* reported that Mother Teresa's home for abandoned children had received a baby that a woman had retrieved from a Calcutta garbage dump. The child had been kept alive by a pack of wild dogs who maintained an all-night vigil to protect the infant and keep him warm. It was found by the woman the following morning.

The *New Mexican* published a report of a pueblo woman who was lost in the desert on Christmas night. In the darkness, she fell twenty-five feet. Hurt and weak, she managed to drag herself into a nearby cave where a dog of mixed breed found her and stayed with her throughout the night. The next day she crawled to the nearest house about a mile in Chimayo. It was the home of Pig Man, the dog that had helped her.

A couple in Massachusetts befriended a stray cat only to have it save them from near catastrophe when a gas burner was left on in the kitchen overnight. The cat mewed so loudly that the woman followed the cat into the room where she saw the burner and corrected the problem.

The media is filled almost daily with stories of domestic and wild animals doing miraculous things that go beyond animal instincts. A cat, nicknamed Scarlet by firemen, returned six times to a burning building to retrieve all of her helpless kittens. Scarlet's fur and skin were badly burned, but she did not stop until all the kittens were safe. A female Rotweiller sniffed out and finally found puppies that had been buried alive by a cruel and insensitive owner. She managed to dig them all up before they suffocated. A cat woke its owner in the middle of the night because her kitten had crawled onto a dangerously narrow ledge. A man adopted a kitten much to his older cat's dismay, but on their first night together, the older cat saved the kitten from drowning in the toilet.

Are these simply survival instincts or something more?

Are animals compassionate, feeling creatures, not unlike ourselves, capable of cruelty, joy and self-sacrifice? Most animal lovers would resound, "Of course!" Every pet owner I ever met, including the scores of people from across the country who were interviewed for this book, has been eager to volunteer stories of his or her pet's sensitive, caring and intuitive nature.

Most of us are familiar with KoKo the gorilla who received widespread attention for her amazing relationship with her "pet" kitten whom she named All Ball in sign language. Many horses befriend goats when they are lonely, and I saw a dolphin at the San Diego Zoo happily share a tank with its "pet" penguin. The penguin used its fin to hold onto the dolphin as they swam together with dance-like grace. It was a magnificent display of beauty and friendship.

Is there more to an animal's emotional make-up than what is currently understood? Do we as animal lovers simply ascribe our human feelings to animals and anthropomorphize them? This question is well posed in Jeffrey Moussaieff Masson's book, *When Elephants Weep, The Emotional Lives of Animals:*

> "The greatest obstacle in science to investigating the emotions of other animals has been an inordinate desire to avoid anthropomorphism. Anthropomorphism means the ascription of human characteristics - thoughts, feelings, consciousness, and motivation - to the nonhuman. When people claim that the elements are conspiring to ruin the picnic or that a tree is their friend, they are anthropomorphizing. Few believe that the weather is plotting against them, but anthropomorphic ideas about animals are held more widely. Outside scientific circles, it is common to speak of thoughts and feelings of pets and of wild and captive animals. Yet many scientists regard even the notion that animals feel pain as the grossest sort of anthropomorphic error."

As a non-scientist, I am granted many freedoms that the scientific community does not have. This does not discount the value of the scientific approach and its undisputable contribution to society. However, I am deeply grateful to pioneers such as Masson who dare to explore the emotional lives of animals despite the possible backlash from colleagues. Joseph Mortenson's *Whale Songs and Wasp Maps, The Mystery of Animal Thinking* explores the animal mind. In his own words, "The drab, dark, mechanistic world of the behaviorist is beginning to be illuminated by the bright light of animal consciousness."

With more explorers such as these diving feet first into the unknown realm of animal consciousness, we may be on the brink of a new era of understanding. Science may have to shift it's perceptions of the animal kingdom and, therefore, be forced to explore questions which up until now have been considered taboo.

Animals Serve

"All our history is his industry. We are his heirs, he our inheritance."
- To The Horse, Ronald Duncan

Throughout history animals have played an important role in serving the human family. Evidence points to the domestication of horses in Eurasia 5,000-6,000 years ago, near the end of the Neolithic period. The dog was domesticated perhaps 6,000 years earlier,(1) and the domestication of the cat, considered sacred in Egypt, most likely began there about 4,000 years ago. It was not until Christianity replaced the Egyptian pantheon that the cat became domesticated in Europe.(2)

Archaeological evidence dating back to the Pleistocene era (about 12,000 years ago) suggests the domestication of dogs began in the area presently known as the Middle East.(3) In northern Israel, the skeleton of a dog was discovered buried with a person's arm around it, suggesting a bond between them.

During the Roman period, dogs were used primarily to catch game. The Middle Ages record the use of dogs in combat with special breeds developed for their loyalty and ferocity. In his book *Dogs*, Don Harper recalls the legend of Gelert, an ancient story that illustrates the loyalty of Irish Wolf Hounds and their ability to defend family members to their death. He writes:

> "Gelert, an Irish Hound, was left guarding a baby while his owner Llewelyn went hunting. On his return, Llewelyn was horrified to be greeted by the sight of an overturned cot, stained blood, and the presence of blood on Gelert's face and body. He killed the dog instantly with his sword, at which point, he heard the baby cry out from under the cot. On venturing further into the room, Llewelyn found the baby unharmed, and the body of a wolf nearby. Horrified by his actions, Llewelyn was reputed to have buried the dog close to his lodge at the village of Beddgelert in Wales, marking the spot with a cairn of stones."

In the early 1600s, it was commonplace to see dogs in church. Special benches were placed at the rear of many churches to accommodate them and their owners. This practice ended dramatically in 1666 at the height of the Great Plague of London. Dogs had infected people with the fleas spread to them by rats. Official dog killers were used to destroy more than 40,000 canines. The 1700s saw a renewal of the domestication of dogs. The population's love and pride in their dogs brought about the first dog show in 1775.(4) Today, with 350 breeds of dogs in the world, the animal's role continues to evolve and expand as its relationship with humanity deepens.

The twentieth century has seen the creation of a new role for animals, dogs especially, including the role of therapy and service dog. Service dogs provide people with special needs. Guide dogs for the blind, while the most commonly known, are by no means the only type of service dogs employed. There are, for example, service dogs for the hearing disabled and assistance dogs for people in wheelchairs. They are trained to alert owners to doorbells, telephones and fire alarms, pick up dropped items, turn on light switches, and much more. Seizure-alert animals have an ability to sense an impending seizure and can alert their owners or health care staff.

Cat Fancy magazine's October 1995 issue carried a wonderful story about Shoo-Shoo, a ten-year-old Siamese whose owner, Karen Brazelton is hearing impaired and relies on her cats to help her "hear" around the house. Shoo-Shoo was the least helpful to her, so she decided to take him to work. Karen is owner and residential manager of a group home. Not long after Shoo-Shoo was brought to work, he began to exhibit an innate ability to sense when a resident was about to have an epileptic seizure. Even when fast asleep in one room, he was known to get up quickly and dash into the room of someone about to have a seizure. He predicted about ten seizures a month at the home. But Shoo-Shoo's abilities didn't stop there. He began to cry, meowing and circling around a non-speaking resident until finally the resident was hospitalized, at which time they discovered he had liver dysfunction. Shoo-Shoo is perhaps one of those angels with fur who was placed in our midst to help us in ways we are not yet able to help ourselves.

The story of Shoo-Shoo is amazing, but not uncommon. More and more people are speaking out about their experiences with animals. In Masson's book, *When Elephant's Weep*, a family purchased a signal dog to help the hearing-impaired father. Gilly, a border collie, woke the mother on her first night home from the hospital with her new-born baby. Gilly ran back and forth from the mother's bed to the baby's cot until the mother finally got out of bed to check on the baby. The baby was silent and blue, having choked on some mucus. His mother was able to clear his passageway and save his life.(5) How did Gilly know the baby was in distress? The dog had only been trained to alert the owner of doorbells, telephones, and the like.

When two-year-old Xandy was diagnosed with autism, he seemed to live in a solitary world. The child did not speak or communicate in any way and his parents feared for his future. Then a miracle happened. Holly, a Golden Retriever trained to be a companion to people with disabilities, came into Xandy's life. Two years after Holly's arrival, Xandy is able to speak and his parents now refer to him as only developmentally delayed. He plays in the snow with Holly, brushes and holds her, and is with her constantly. The love they share helped Xandy out of his isolation, and into a world of warmth, wonder, and hope.

Animal lovers now have the opportunity to help become a puppy "angel" raiser. Canine Companions, the organization that trained Holly, is looking for puppy raisers to help them raise companion dogs.(6) Information about this and other organizations can be found in the resource section of this book.

It appears that certain animals have a heightened sensitivity that enables them to serve in a very special way. Is this simply an overdeveloped instinct or a God-given gift? Each of us can draw our own conclusions, but remember, there were many things thought to be far-fetched a hundred years ago that are widely accepted today. I believe that we are always being sent help from a power greater than ourselves. The help is there if we learn to say "yes" to it. I am reminded of a statement by James Thurber: "It is better to know some of the questions, than all of the answers."

Animals Heal

*"In the glance of the speechless animal there is a discourse
that only the soul of the wise can
really understand."*
- An Indian Poet

Therapy dogs typically work with their owners in hospitals, nursing homes, schools and rehabilitation centers. They play with abused children, give affection to the elderly, allow the critically ill to laugh and forget their pain for a short while, and sometimes provide a warm lick to wipe the tears away.

Therapy dogs played an important role in the aftermath of the Oklahoma City bombing. Search and rescue dogs were used to locate possible survivors. Therapy dogs and volunteers stayed at the convention center comforting survivors, family members waiting for news of their loved ones, and rescue workers heavily stressed by the work and its emotional strain. People at the convention center hugged the dogs. They laughed and cried with them. One television station taped an exhausted rescue worker who was crying and holding a Golden Retriever.(7)

Eva Shaw, PhD., author of *What to Do When A Loved One Dies*, said: "Because therapy animals, dogs in particular, provide unconditional love, they can be a tremendous help during the grieving process."

Not all therapy animals are dogs. Cats, rabbits, birds and even dolphins work as therapy animals. Sometimes a pet can serve as a therapy pet to its owner. Many studies are now being conducted on the positive health benefits of owning pets. Dr. Erika Friedmann, professor at Brooklyn College, recently studied 350 cardiac patients. Nineteen of the 282 patients who did not own dogs died within one year of the heart attack. Of the 87 patients who did own a dog, only one died. In the *AKC Gazette*, Friedmann pointed out, one reason for this could be that people who own dogs exercise more because they need to walk their pet and are, therefore, healthier than non-pet owners. However, when Dr. Friedmann compared physiological profiles of dog owners and non-dog owners, there were significant differences. "These differences suggested that the relationship itself with the animal was the key predictor of the survival rates."(8)

Rebecca Reynolds, an occupational therapist and author of *Bring Me The Ocean* manages a traveling therapeutic program for healing those confined to health care institutions. She brings various animals and birds to chronically ill patients as a means of connection. The simple affection of these creatures can give people a respite from the pain and isolation that often accompanies severe disease and deformities. As Rebecca points out in a wonderful article in *The Spirit of Change* magazine's May/June 1996 issue:

> "An animal doesn't mind if a person is missing a limb or does not speak. With an animal, we have the opportunity to feel whole, both physically and emotionally, freed for the moment from our misgivings.... Through the human's automatic use of comparison and contrast, the animal is made an intermediary for learning about oneself and, ultimately, about acceptance."

Acceptance and non-judgement are perhaps the two most important gifts that animals can offer us. To these loving animals, we are perfect. Those extra pounds make us all the more cuddly. The wrinkled, arthritic body is overlooked when a puppy jumps up into a new lap. The lessons they teach are simple and, yet, not always easy to learn. The essence of the person and the richness of the moment is where our attention needs to be focused, rather than to dwell on the past or make fearful predictions of the future. Animals exist in the here and now. They can help us emerge from our self-centered world and join them in the simplicity of the moment. As Samuel Butler once observed, "All animals except man know that the ultimate aim of life is to enjoy it."

Dolphins have been depicted as friends of man as far back as the Greeks. There are countless stories of dolphins saving drowning victims or guiding lost ships safely to harbor. During the last twenty years, a group of therapists, doctors and parents have ascribed to dolphins the power to heal. In 1978, an educational anthropologist in Florida, named Betsy Smith, developed a program called "Project InReach" which was designed to study the effects of dolphin play on children who were neurologically impaired, suffered from Down's Syndrome, or autism. In the July/August 1996 issue of *New Age Journal*, "Dr. Dolphin" Smith referred to dolphins as natural healers with peculiar empathy. The article then examines the Dolphin-Human therapy program in Key Largo, Florida run by psychologist David Nathanson. In a study conducted in 1988 and reported in the European research journal *Anthrozoos*, Nathanson worked with children with speech problems using the centers' dolphin protocol. He compared his results with those achieved in a classroom setting. The dolphin treatment was an impressive ten times more effective than the classroom setting.

Dolphin therapy has proven to be effective in boosting the immune system by stimulating the production of T-cells, in relieving stress and, in some cases, even depression. Horace Dobbs is a medical researcher who runs International Dolphin Watch in East Yorkshire, England. Dobbs' research focuses mainly on the dolphin-human interaction and its effects on depression. Dobbs observed that some wild dolphins, whom he calls "ambassador" dolphins, seemed to gravitate toward emotionally-troubled individuals.

David Cole, founder of AquaThought Foundation in Fort Myers, Florida is seeking to understand some of the dolphin's mysterious healing abilities by studying its sonar. Cole monitors the brain waves of people who swim with dolphins.

He has seen that right and left hemispheres, which are normally very different, begin to synchronize. This brain activity is usually associated with heightened awareness and increased learning ability. Dolphins, horses, dogs and cats are being used more and more in therapeutic settings with amazing results.

Tony Award-winning actress, Patricia Elliott (a personal friend), has been enamored with dolphins for the last twenty years. In 1987 she was given the opportunity to swim with dolphins at the Dolphin Research Center in Marathon Key, Florida. Her experience was so profound and life-changing that she went on two more adventures in the ensuing years. She recalled one of her experiences while swimming in Hawaii:

> "We swam out about a half mile from the shore and were hanging on to these buoys when we spotted about 25 of them swimming back and forth, back and forth. We had our fins on, so we went over, and they let us swim with them for about two hours. There was one female who would swim first on one side of me, then the other, checking me out. It was amazing!
>
> "It was an introduction to joy, a reminder that happiness is ever present if only you're receptive to it. For me, the dolphins are angels in not-very-clever disguise. Looking into their eyes is like falling into God. I've been doing spiritual work for years with things like meditation, and I felt myself take a big leap forward in my progress after these encounters."

Serious research on the healing effects of the human-animal connection is proving time and time again that there is a magical, unexplained quality to this special relationship. Could some of these silent intermediaries be angels in fur or fins, sent to help us with our pain and struggles, and to encourage us to stop and embrace the moment with love, care and acceptance?

Animals Teach

But ask now the beasts, and they shall teach thee;
and the fowls of the air, and they shall tell thee.
Or speak to the Earth, and it shall tell thee:
- Job 12:7.8 KJV

Psychologist Karen Allen, of the State University of New York School of Medicine at Buffalo, conducted a study of the calming effects of pets on their owners in stressful situations. She tested 240 couples, half of them dog owners, as they performed three stressful tasks. The smallest increases in blood pressure and heart rate were achieved when the person was alone with the pet. Ironically, spouses proved to be the least comforting. Dr. Allen believes, "Dogs are like your husband or wife on a good day. They're nonjudgmental and always glad to see you."(9)

At first glance this book may appear to be a simple and heartwarming study reflecting our love of animals, but I see it as a great deal more than that. It goes to the core of the issue of lifestyle and meaning.

Stress is the number one killer of human beings in this country. We live in an increasingly technological age where stress and competition are common-place. Stress is so widely diagnosed that many of us become desensitized to its seriousness. We take aspirin for that tension headache, sleeping pills to sleep, caffeine to wake, our beloved sugar to comfort, and then seek the simulated effects of love and care from the endorphins in our chocolate bars.

Most of us can relate to this behavior to a greater or lesser degree, but have we ever stopped to examine the craziness of it? Where is the priority of joy and love in such an existence? As Masson points out in his article, "The Emotional Lives of Animals," (*New Age Magazine*, March/ April 1995):

> "A principal source of joy for social animals is the presence of their family and the members of their group. Nim Chimpsky, a chimpanzee, was raised in a human family for the first year and a half of his life. When he was about four years old, a reunion was arranged with the family who raised him. When he spotted them, in a place where he had never seen them before, Nim smiled hugely, shrieked, and pounded the ground for three minutes, gazing back and forth at the different members of the family. Finally he calmed down enough to go and hug his foster mother, still smiling, and shrieking intermittently. He spent more than an hour hugging his family, grooming them and playing with them before they left. This was the only occasion on which Nim was seen to smile for more than a few minutes."

Are we so different? What makes us smile and feel like jumping for joy? Is love any less healing and comforting if its source is not human? On the contrary, according to a study done at the Waltham Center for Pet Nutrition in Leicestershire, England, a pet's love can help its owner reduce anxiety, lower blood pressure and triglyceride levels, moderate the effects of stress, and build a sense of empathy. Seventy percent of the study's participants reported an increase in family happiness after getting a pet. Love, human or otherwise, creates a bond that undeniably aids in the health, happiness and sense of belonging that makes life worth living.

Pets help us to slow down. They help us stop and smell the roses. Taking the time to walk the dog, stroke your adoring kitty, or ride your beloved horse on a frosty morning, helps us to shift away from the demands in our lives and enjoy the simplicity of nature and companionship. Balance in all things is the key to harmony and health. How fortunate we humans are to have loving pets to help us transcend the pressures of modern life. If our pets are our teachers, then perhaps the most important lesson they have to teach us is to love ourselves and others, as they love us.

I once heard a prayer that I have used as a barometer for my own emotional self-esteem. "I pray that I may become the person that my dog thinks I am. I pray that I may learn to love others as unconditionally and non-judgmentally as she loves me." Mark Twain's anecdote lends levity to this truth. "Heaven goes by favor. If it went by merit, you would stay out, and your dog would go in."

Animals Know

Your friend is your needs answered.
He is your field which you sow with love and reap with
    thanksgiving.
And he is your board and your fireside.
For you come to him with your hunger, and you seek him
    for peace."
    - The Prophet, Kahlil Gibran

What is this bond between animals and human beings? For some, it is a love that is deeper and more profound than with human beings. Many people relate to their animals as their children or best friend, and care for them with that intensity and devotion.   Animals have been known to sacrifice their own lives to protect their masters. Throughout history and in all cultures there are heartbreaking stories of dogs mourning at the grave of their departed master, even to the point of starvation.

The animal's devotion for man is cited by Darwin when he wrote, "In the agony of death a dog has been known to caress his master, and every one has heard of the dog suffering under vivisection who licked the hand of the operator; this man, unless the operation was fully justified by an increase of our knowledge, or unless he had a heart of stone, must have felt remorse to the last hour of his life."

In India, the Bodhisattva Avalokitesvara is depicted with a thousand hands. The story tells of Avalokitesvara who, having lived a good life, enters Nirvana when he sees an animal in pain. He is so moved by the poor suffering creature that he asks his father if he can stay and help. He knows in his heart he would have no peace in Heaven if he left the wounded animal unaided. Father gave his blessing and granted him a thousand eyes to see and a thousand hands to help all the suffering animals in the kingdom.

> *"In safety and in Bliss*
> *May all creatures be of a blissful heart*
> *Whatever breathing beings there may be*
> *Frail or firm...long or big...short or small*
> *Seen or unseen, dwelling far or near*
> *Existing or yet seeking to exist*
> *May all creatures be of a blissful heart."*
> *- Sutta Nipata*

Few of us will argue about the loving bond that we have with our animals, but is there also an intuitive bond? Do animals have a telepathic link with those they love? British biologist, Rupert Sheldrake, who received hundreds of letters from pet owners with tales of pet telepathy, believes that there is. Sheldrake states: "The only way to explain these behaviors is to suppose that there is an invisible link or psychic bond between people and their animals, through which influences can be communicated at a distance." Sheldrake gives an example of a widowed neighbor's cat who always knew when her son, a merchant marine, was coming home from the sea, even if he had not written to say when he was arriving. The cat would sit on the front door mat and meow for an hour or two before he arrived. This let her know when to start tea for him.

There appears to be a sixth sense with animals. Animal behaviorist, Roger Mugford told the *London Sunday Telegraph*, "Animals have many different senses from humans. They can detect very low frequency sounds and geomagnetic changes, so it should not surprise us if they can sense things we can't." He concludes, "I don't think we need to invent a sixth sense. They just combine their many senses more effectively."

Based on his preliminary research, Sheldrake believes that normal senses cannot adequately explain what is happening. He explains that the nature of the bond between people and their pets is linked to what he calls a morphic field. "In my hypothesis of morphic resonance, I propose that invisible fields shape the way organisms grow, organize the instincts of animals, and underlie their social bonds. I suggest that influences can travel within this field, just as radio and TV transmissions travel within the electromagnetic field."

Sheldrake is well aware of the controversy that exists around the existence of morphic fields, but he concludes, "If they exist, then invisible influences passing from person to animal and vice-versa could explain these uncanny powers of pets." (Note: Information on pet telepathy research can be found in the organization section of this book).(10)

How do pets know when their owner is returning home? Are pets truly telepathic? Is this ability based on an invisible link with humanity, as Sheldrake believes, or is Sheldrake's hypothesis only partially true? Is this link, in fact, spiritual in nature and far beyond even the parameters of parapsychology? Are some animals sent to us as guardian angels to love, protect and comfort us in our times of need?

I, for one, have known this aid and comfort. It has lifted me up beyond the walls of my limited perception to a glimpse of Divine Grace. As all of us who have known a special pet can testify, angels with fur exist and their existence blesses us.

"Hear our humble prayer, O God, for our friends the animals, especially for animals who are suffering; for any that are hunted or lost, or deserted or frightened or hungry; for all that must be put to death. We entreat for them all thy mercy and pity... Make us, ourselves, to be true friends to animals and so to share the blessings of the merciful."
- Albert Schweitzer

Chapter Two

Beloved Beast

Teach me the soulful dance of quiet, unconditional love.
The heart rhythm that heals all pain.
Teach me the hawk's winged fancy that lets go freely
to the whims of the mighty wind.
Teach me to fill my heart completely
holding nothing back even if bursting and broken it
comes to be.
Teach me to be more like you, old, gentle beast
As wise as any I've ever known.
Teach me to mourn you proudly with dignity and honor.
To model your sphinx-like grace that heaven's gate will
now adorn.
Teach me to trust that love does not end with death,
And that you will run to greet me when I pass through the
veil.
-Santi Meunier, Summer, 1996
For Tosha, my teacher and faithful companion.

My Angel With Fur

By
Pamela Santi Meunier

I grew up with dogs as a child and preferred their company to that of most humans. Dogs weren't complicated. You could count on them. In those turbulent years growing up, it was the steadfast, unconditional love of my dog, Tara, that kept me going. Losing her was like having my favorite color suddenly erased from the face of the earth, never to be seen again. My memory strained to remember the joy of her presence, but with nothing to compare it to, it eventually was lost in the gray bleakness of my grief.

My parents died not long after Tara. In fact, it was one loss after another until I found myself with no family to speak of and no more pets to share my home. I devoted my time to building a career, traveling, and trying to find Mr. Right. At a very young age, I was determined that my life was not going to be a wasted one. I wanted to see the world, have adventures, and experience as much as I could. By the time I was 30, I was ready to settle down. I had moved to the Berkshires in Massachusetts, to a small farm located twenty-seven miles from the nearest market. A farm meant animals, flowers, fresh grown vegetables, and best of all, a dog! My dream was to find a pure-bred Golden Retriever, preferably a female, so I could raise puppies. Before long the neighbors up the street announced that their Goldens had mated and, knowing my dream, offered me the pick of the litter. Few things have given me more delight than fat, fluffy puppies. I was overjoyed. After many years of struggling through life's hardships, it felt as if all my dreams were coming true.

The longest weeks of my life were spent that summer waiting for Cleo's litter to be born. When her due week finally came, I rushed home from work each night and went straight up to their house to see if the puppies had arrived. Cleo got fatter and fatter, and looked as if she would burst if she had to wait one more minute. But each day would pass and still nothing. Einstein was right. Time is relative. It has certainly been my experience that the things you want most take forever to arrive, and the things you dread are here in a flash.

The call came early one morning while I was stumbling around the kitchen making coffee. Cleo had given birth to eleven healthy, hungry puppies. I dropped everything and ran up the street. What a sight! They were all curled around each other like caramel taffy while Cleo sat on guard, trying not to nod off from exhaustion. I sat on the floor next to the whelping box and watched them whimper and squirm, sleeping in the safety of their mother's warmth. Susie, Cleo's owner, was kind enough to bring me a cup of coffee. She had been up all night with the delivery but, like me, was too excited to go to bed. We sat on the floor in the mud room and watched the miracle of newborn life.

I cannot be certain if my eyes were drawn to one particular puppy, or if this puppy drew my gaze to her. Nevertheless, once I saw her and stroked her little back, I knew she was the one. "That is my puppy. That is the one I want." Susie looked at me quizzically and said, "They were just born. You have weeks to go before you need to make a decision. Why not wait until they are about a month old when their personalities will begin to emerge?" Her words fell on deaf ears. This was my puppy, the one that I had waited for since Tara's death almost twenty years before. I gently placed my large hand on her small back and told her she was my girl, that I would visit her every day until it was time to come home with me. She was only three hours old when we found each other. I know Susie did not take me seriously and assumed that when the time came, I would pick the cutest puppy and that would be it. But I never did change my mind. I couldn't because the decision wasn't actually made by me. It was merely shown to me. She was my girl and there would be no parting us from that moment on.

Ripe pumpkins and a few gourds were all that was left of the summer garden when Tosha came home with me. The fall air held a particular bite to it that signaled the onset of winter. Winters are long in the Berkshire's, but this winter I would have my puppy to keep me company. Tosha was a great companion because her presence filled the room. When Tosha was inside, all attention was focused on her. Even friends who weren't particularly fond of animals loved her. She soon acquired a following of admirers who would take her camping, hiking, swimming, and sledding. She was happy and in turn, made everyone around her happy. This was a gift I thought all Goldens possess, and to a certain extent, I think this is true. But Tosha had something more, and that "something" was revealed to me increasingly over the years.

Tosha's enthusiasm taught me to soak up the essence of each moment, to not hold back, or postpone for later, the joy awaiting our reunions. Her sphinx-like patience and groundedness demonstrated a level of trust and acceptance that I sorely lacked. The most important quality, I was privileged to witness over the fourteen years we spent together, was a loving tenderness so sweet that I have come to regard it as angelic. There are countless heartwarming examples, but the one that comes to mind is a story I was blessed to witness, but almost didn't.

Tosha and I lived with two cats, Sufi and Niki. It was a beautiful spring day, the animals were outside in the yard and I was preparing lunch. All of a sudden, I heard an ungodly screech, and a few moments later, the sound of cats howling and scampering off into the woods. I rushed to the window to see what had happened. To my horror, the cats had trapped and killed a young baby rabbit. Outraged, Tosha chased the cats from their prey. Ever so gently, she picked up the limp, little bunny in her mouth and carried it across the yard to the edge of the woods. There, she gently placed the bunny on the ground and dug a deep hole. With slow, methodical care, she placed the rabbit in the hole and proceeded to cover it up. Tosha then stood by the grave as if to say a prayer and a final good-bye. After a while she turned away, and went back to her favorite spot in the shade for her nap.

I stood in awe at what I had witnessed. It was then that I began to think of Tosha as my angel with fur.

Our journey together was filled with painful challenges as well as joys. I am reminded of the time when I was very ill with female problems and the news that I would not be able to bear children cut through me like a knife. My husband and I separated and many friends proved not to be friends, but Tosha always stayed close and steadfast. I feel in my heart that she was sent so that I could get through those painful years. It has been said that angels appear and answer our prayers when we remember to ask for their help. I believe, without a doubt, that she was sent as my answer.

The ironic part of our relationship is that even when I appeared to be helping her, in retrospect, I came to understand that she was truly helping me. A perfect illustration of this was when Tosha was pregnant. When I discovered that I was sterile, I transferred all of my maternal instincts to her and the prospect of having a litter of puppies. I found her the perfect mate, and when she was in heat, I bred them. She was young and had excellent papers, as did the sire, and everyone excitedly awaited the blessed event. I did everything by the book: made the perfect welping box, saved lots of newspapers, and fed her beef liver, egg and rice omelets. Nothing was too much trouble for her and her puppies. She was in "hog heaven", or I should say "dog heaven". She was as big as a house when her due date arrived. Up until then, Tosha was frisky and appeared in good health.

We were in the kitchen and I was making my morning coffee when suddenly Tosha stood up and her water broke. The kitchen floor flooded with a foul-smelling green liquid. For the first time in her life, Tosha looked scared. When I called the vet and described the situation, he became very alarmed. He asked me to carefully put her in the car and get to his office as fast as I could. Tosha was very large. Even before her pregnancy, she weighed 82 pounds of solid muscle. Now she must have weighed over 100 pounds. How could I possibly lift her into the car? I took a few deep breaths, said a prayer, and looking Tosha right in the eye, I told her no matter how hard or painful it was, she had to help me do this. Her courageous spirit never let me down, and it did not then. It almost killed her, but she got into the car.

The vet explained that her entire litter of eleven puppies was dead. He had to surgically remove the sack very carefully because if it burst before he could get it out, she would die. He told me gravely that she only had a slim chance of surviving, and that he would do his best.

The operation took six hours. It seemed more like six days as I sat in the waiting room, praying she would not be taken from me. I had come to rely on her presence. She was my anchor and my closest friend.

Much to the vet's amazement, she pulled through. The long operation left her slightly brain-damaged and sterile, but I didn't care. I had my girl back and that was all that mattered. I was able to bring Tosha home in about a week. I expected her to be the same as she had been before, but she was not. Her head hung low. She didn't want to go for a walk or even take a swim. No matter what I did, I could not cheer her up. I finally called the vet and told him about her behavior. I wasn't sure if this was the brain-damage that he had talked about. He assured me she was simply depressed, that maybe if I went to the store and bought a stuffed animal to substitute for her lost litter, she might snap out of it. I was willing to try, although I couldn't imagine it actually working.

It was Easter and the only animals in the store were bunnies. I hoped it wouldn't matter that it wasn't a puppy. I chose a big white one with long ears. Tosha always greeted me at the door, but this time was different. After weeks of being listless and deeply depressed, Tosha took one look at the Easter bunny, gleefully grabbed it out of my hand, and pranced off with it to her bed in a tail-wagging frenzy. She had become her happy, loving self again, and in that instant, her joy returned. She had a baby to love and care for, and that was all she wanted. Since then, I have given her a "baby" every Christmas, and everyone of them is greeted warmly like that first time. She loves, cares for, and grooms it, and when company comes over, she proudly displays it to all the guests. When I discovered I would never have children, I experienced a tremendous loss. I felt barren and without purpose. Interestingly, it was Tosha who supported me most through that painful time, and then, ironically, she went through it herself. She taught me a most valuable lesson; to mourn what is lost, but to love and cherish what I have.

Tosha and I carried on with our lives and I wish I could say that after her loss and mine, life went on smoothly, but that was not the case. Several years passed and I began to notice a slight shift in Tosha's energy level. It was subtle at first, but became steadily more pronounced. One morning, she did not want to go for her walk. Instead, she just looked at me as if to say, "I am too tired. Please don't make me go." I took her to the vet to determine what was wrong, but he felt that without extensive tests and some blood work, a diagnosis was not possible. Over the years, Tosha and I developed a strong communication. She didn't "speak" to me often, but when she did it was loud, clear, and unmistakable. This was one of those times. Tosha did not want to go through any tests.

Years before when I was sick with endometriosis, I had seen a healer and an herbalist who had been helpful and supportive. I thought if anyone could help Tosha, she could. Her diagnosis was almost immediate, and it confirmed my worst suspicions. Tosha had leukemia. The healer suggested drastic treatment, which involved giving Tosha a poisonous herb. She said it would either kill the cancer or kill her. In her opinion, it was Tosha's only hope.

At first I was vehemently against it. I loved her too much to take the chance that I could actually be poisoning her. I was so bonded with Tosha that the thought of losing her made me collapse in tears. I did not feel strong enough to take this course of action. I asked God to give me the courage to do what was best for her, regardless of how I felt. I asked Tosha what she wanted me to do. I felt her say in her sweet and simple way, "There is happiness in death, and there is happiness in life, but there is no happiness in this sickness.

Don't hold onto me." Tearfully, I took in her words and her wisdom. I went to bed knowing that the next morning, I would let her treatment begin. Letting go of those I love has been a big part of my life's learning. In that day's sorrow, I was reminded once again that I do not own anything, not even myself, and that it is all on loan from God.

In my dreams that night, I had the most beautiful vision. Tosha was sleeping in her favorite, shady spot outside the door to my office and an angel appeared overhead. The angel circled the rooftop several times, and then floated down and effortlessly picked Tosha's spirit up and off they both flew into the clouds. Tosha's golden body remained looking peacefully asleep on the warm grass. This vision of Tosha's death gave me a sense of peace. It was so vivid that, upon waking, I took out my easel and painted it. The painting took several hours, and when it was complete, I gave Tosha her first dose of medicine. As I stirred it into her food, I told her that no matter what happened she was the most precious thing in all the world to me, a gift from God. I would not, however, let my needs infringe upon her freedom in any way. She was free to go, if it was her time. I would not hold her back.

The treatment plan took six weeks. It consisted of daily hands-on healing treatments which I administered twice a day. Those six weeks were long and arduous. One day she would appear to get better, only to relapse on the next. I had no idea what would happen. I only knew that during this period, I had learned something that previously I had only experienced on the surface. I knew unconditional love, the kind that has no expectation and needs no recognition. It is loving for the pure joy of loving, a complete act that needs nothing. I finally began to experience what a great teacher of mine once said, "Love is the reward for loving." I finally understood what she meant.

Tosha miraculously survived and recovered fully. Once again she could run, swim and eat all of her dinner. I have known joy because of Tosha and I have known unconditional love. Her sweetness eludes description, but the effects are clearly seen on anyone who has come in contact with her.

Tosha is now fourteen years old. Her hips are riddled with arthritis and a stroke has left her blind in one eye. She is leaving me slowly, like a summer sunset that spreads colors across the sky when the sun is still high in the west. Each day I say good-bye, not knowing if it will be our last, but I have kept my promise to her. I will not hold her. She knows she is loved, and free to go.

All that is left to say is, "Dear friend, you are all that is fine, good, and loving in this world. God must be very proud of you. You have done your job well. No one could have done better. Bless you, old girl."

God sent me an angel, an angel with fur, and I have been lifted up by it.

Tosha passed away quietly on Thanksgiving weekend 1999 and was buried in the backyard under a dogwood tree with a stone angel to mark the spot. Our other dog, Niki, is often seen sleeping there in the afternoon.

Chapter Three

"...And so it is you cheer me
My old friend,
For to know you and be near you,
My old friend
Makes my hopes of clearer light,
And my faith of surer sight,
And soul a purer white,
My old friend."
- James Whitcomb Reily

Motors

By
Marty Klein

My cat died on August 25, 1990. He lived 19 years, 5 months and 10 days. That's significant because no living thing ever lived with me longer than Motors did. He watched me go through many changes as a human being. Who knows how aware animals really are, and whether we'll ever truly understand their unique perception of the world. I think my cat always knew what was going on regarding the changes in our lives. He was special.

I met Motors the same day I met Ellen, the woman I was to marry. When Ellen brought me back to her little cottage that first day in April 1971, she warned me about her cats. She said her mother hated cats so she always kept some of them around, just to make sure her mother would stay away.

When I walked into her small, two-room home, I couldn't believe my eyes: Twenty-one cats! They were everywhere. I mean, everywhere; on every chair and table, under every cabinet and dresser, on the stove, on top of the refrigerator, in the closet, and even in the bathtub. There was no part of her house that didn't have a cat in it, on it, or around it. I didn't like cats at all, so for me this was quite an adjustment. My only connection to cats during my whole life was hearing the alley cats fight at night between apartment houses in Brooklyn. I never did anything mean to cats, like some of the other kids in the neighborhood did. They'd throw rocks at cats, sometimes run after them and try to kick them. I never tried to hurt them. I just didn't like them.

Ellen explained that she really only had four cats. Two of them just had litters of 8 and 9, respectively; hence, 21 cats. I understood math, but when we went to sleep I had to keep pushing the never-ending tide of kittens off my body. Cats everywhere! Give me a break!! I didn't get much sleep that night.

There was one persistent kitten that wouldn't leave me alone. All night long he kept climbing up my body to the same spot--my head. I'd be sleeping on my stomach and he would nuzzle in my hair and fall asleep. I kept pushing him off, but would continually wake up to find him all tangled in my hair and purring quietly. He was so determined to be close to me, that by morning, in spite of my efforts to the contrary, we had become friends.

That afternoon Ellen and I were on her sofa trying to listen to a record album she had put on. The same little kitten who had slept in my hair was staring at the record going round and round when, all of a sudden, he leapt onto the revolving turntable, right on the record, and began spinning around with it in circles. The needle flew off and scratched the record as Ellen yelled and grabbed the kitten. At that point. I was hooked. I became hysterical, laughing so hard that tears ran down my face. I knew that little guy just had to be something special. I scooped him up and placed him in my lap. He never stopped purring. So we named him Motors. That was April 27, 1971.

A few weeks later, Ellen and I moved into a fifth floor, upscale apartment house in Coconut Grove. If the cats got out of our apartment, they could run for a good distance through the carpeted hallway. They always tried to sneak out just for fun and because they were curious. It was always a great adventure whenever one of the three cats would outsmart us. I remember once Motors snuck out and ran down the hall, only to find a huge Great Dane and his master walking in the opposite direction. Motors stopped cold, but didn't run away. He just stood there, as if defying the Dane to do something. The Dane's master said he never saw such a courageous cat.

A couple of weeks later, a friend stopped by with her dog, a mutt who weighed about 30 or 40 pounds. Motors was in the bedroom with me and the dog happened to wander in. When they noticed each other, Motors got down off the bed, eased up to the mutt while hissing and hauled off with two quick rights to the nose of the unsuspecting canine. The dog rolled over, yelping in pain, crashed into the closet and ran out of the room as fast as he could. Was this a sweet little kitten I had, or some kind of a feline freak! I didn't know, but I was downright impressed with the little warrior in him. Actually, I felt quite proud. I've always cheered for the underdog and in my mind any cat that could beat up on a dog was surpassing the odds. I went out and bought him a quarter pound of shrimp. This was my cat and I felt proud.

Motors had a unique quality he picked up from his mother. If we left a glass of milk or water on the table, he would sit next to it and, one paw at a time, scoop up the liquid and lick it off his paw. He used to do this when we gave him the remains of a container of yogurt. I would watch him endlessly, fascinated by his adeptness. While he licked and pawed, he'd be purring to beat the band.

When we moved to Albuquerque in the summer of 1972, we drove across the south in our big van with the three cats. The other two cats were pretty miserable the whole trip, but Motors was hanging out in my lap, enjoying the adventure. Every now and then, he would place his front paws on the dashboard with his back paws on my legs and then stand real tall and stare out the window. People in passing cars just couldn't believe it. They always pointed at him. Well, when's the last time you had a cat staring back at you while driving down the road?

We settled in Albuquerque and within three months bought a house. This was significant for Motors because he finally got to experience freedom. A sliding glass door at the back of the house opened onto our backyard, which consisted of some grass, a few trees and lots of weeds and dirt. The neighboring houses were separated by stone walls about four feet high. All three cats were constantly scratching on the glass door crying to be let out. Ellen's biggest fear was that they would run in all directions and never come back. After finally coaxing her to loosen up with them, we opened the door. The other two cats slowly stepped outside like well-behaved felines, sniffing and exploring very carefully. Not Motors. He bolted out the door, rolled in the soft dirt, leapt into the air and proceeded to scramble up one of the smaller trees. Ellen tried to chase him, but it was a joke. No way was he going to wait around to get picked up and brought back to the house. He loved his freedom. Whenever Ellen got close he would dart away. I managed to talk Ellen into letting him be, and as soon as she stopped her frantic behavior, he stopped his wild reactions. Eventually he came in, but he would never again settle for being an indoor cat. He seemed to live out my philosophy of life. Or maybe I wished I could experience the same freedom Motors enjoyed. At any rate, I definitely identified with him and we were solid friends. I had myself a great cat and I was in love with him.

We actually had many names for Motors. Whatever we

called him was usually based on the circumstances of the moment. He was neutered in Albuquerque and after the operation, his stomach sagged. Everybody used to think "he" was a "she" and "she" looked pregnant. "When is she going to have babies?" we used to hear all the time. When we explained that "she" was really a "he", people reacted with "Wow, he's really fat!" Hence, his first nickname, Fat Cat. Over the following months, it would shift to Fat Man and Fatto, always said by people with smiles on their faces. That year while in Albuquerque, I wrote a song about my cat and called him Motor Man, and it would come out like "the Motor Man"--lots of names to describe one very interesting little, or maybe not so little, cat!

Ellen got me a beautiful white, male shepherd for my birthday. I named him "Bucky" after the name of the great dog in Jack London's book *The Call of the Wild.* When we brought him home, he was 5 weeks old and weighed only 5 pounds. He was a real sweetie pie, but the cats didn't have the same reaction towards him. He always wanted to play with them, but they wanted nothing to do with him. The other two cats would hiss and scamper away whenever he came around, but not Motors. Motors was the disciplinarian. He made sure Bucky knew who was boss. When Bucky came near, Motors would pepper his nose with between 5 and 10 smacks until the puppy would retreat dazed and confused with a bloody snout. That training developed Bucky's permanent respect for the power of his feline brother. Later, when Bucky grew into a big strapping 100-pound powerhouse, he always approached Motors with caution. They turned out to be the best of friends.

At the time, our lives seemed so scattered that the only love and stability for us was our animals. We got another white shepherd, this time a female, bought and sold a house, moved to Chester, New York, then to Woodstock and back to Miami, all in a period of eighteen months. We were truckin' and it was nuts!

I was in the process of losing my sight. By the time we rented a home in the Coral Gables section of Miami, my vision had gotten really bad, but I could still see Motors. I remember sitting on the couch one afternoon with Motors in my lap. The angle of the sun must have been just right because when I looked down, I could see his eyes so clearly. He looked up at me and we stared at each other. It was wonderful to, once again, experience eye contact with another living creature. I wanted to stop time and for a few minutes, it did. We just stared into the depths of our beings. Then the angle of the sun shifted and the next scene in my life took over. That was the last time I ever made eye contact, but the memory of that moment remains as clear as a bell in my mind.

We moved again a year later, this time back up to Woodstock. That summer Ellen's parents came to visit and they brought along their two shepherds. We had to work carefully to allow each set of dogs out without fighting. One morning we forgot that Motors was outside. Ellen's mom's female shepherd caught Motors by surprise and rushed at him. Motors ran towards the woods, but the shepherd caught him and picked him up in her mouth, trying to rip him apart. This took all of two minutes and while it occurred, our dogs went crazy as Ellen and I frantically ran towards the disaster area. Ellen lunged at the dog and got Motors loose just in the nick of time. A few more seconds and I think my kitty cat would have been a goner. Motor Man survived, but he was really shaken from the episode and never again acted boldly outside the house. It broke my heart to see him run and hide at the sound of dogs in the distance. But I still had my Motor Man.

When Ellen and I separated in 1977, we agreed to split up the four animals we had at the time. Ellen kept the two females, one cat and one dog, and I kept Motors and Bucky. The three of us moved into a simple two bedroom house and the bonds between us grew like never before. Neither Motors or Bucky had their old friends so they started spending a lot more time around each other. They had such a beautiful respect for one another. Motors came to expect that his big brother would protect him from other dogs and Bucky did just that. However, Motors did not venture too far when Bucky was not outside. They would often sleep in bed with me and, many times in passing, Motors would give Bucky a lick on his nose. Sometimes Bucky would come in from the rain all soaked and would lie down with his head flat on the living room floor. Motors would come over and for three or four minutes he would slowly lick Bucky's face dry. God, were they incredible! I felt so blessed to have two such animals to live with. Who said cats and dogs can't get along.

Inherent in my little kitty was the ability to hunt and capture prey. He would proudly bring back his apprehended creatures and plop them down right by the front door. He caught birds and mice mostly, but occasionally he'd wander back with a snake or even a baby rabbit. It used to disturb me, especially when the victims were still very much alive. Once in the middle of the night, he meandered into my bedroom and dropped a live mouse at the foot of my bed. The mouse tried to get away and Motors started chasing him all over the room. I leaped up from a deep sleep, and started yelling, ran out of the bedroom, shut the door to keep the mouse cornered, put my big galoshes on, hurriedly tossed a winter jacket over my naked body, found a broom, and proceeded to march back in the bedroom ready for combat. I ran in, shut the door, paused for a confused moment, and started laughing out of control. I got a glimpse of my battle uniform and could not keep it together There I was, naked with boots and jacket and broom running around chasing a dying mouse. I always had Motors to thank for bringing out my most bizarre behavior.

Motors, Bucky and I used to sit in the sun on the front stoop during the colder months. I would sit cross-legged with Motors curled up in my lap and Bucky would be lying down on the step below. Every so often Motors would stand up, stretch for a few seconds and go curl up so close to Bucky

that their fur would be touching. Neighbors walking by
would just stop and stare. Some would make a point of
saying how delightful and fascinating it was to see "that dog
and cat of yours being so friendly to each other." Those kinds
of comments always brought tears of joy to my eyes. I was so
proud of them.

I had such a deep connection with my cat. I was always
in fear of him dying or disappearing and never coming back.
Bucky represented my outer personality and Motors my inner
workings. Bucky was like my defense and protection against
the harsh world out there, but Motors was like the little boy
within, being innocent, vulnerable, creative, and playful. I
needed the Motor Man for so many reasons that to live
without him would have been devastating. I let him love me
and I expressed much loving, caring, and nurturing towards
this furry little creature. My friends used to say I was his
mother, and I liked that. I cried many times thinking that his
temporary absence meant he was gone forever. Once I found
myself crying in bed thinking he was dead. I wasn't sure if he
had gone out and not come back or if he was missing
somewhere in the house. All I knew was that he was nowhere
to be found. After frantically searching in vain, I stopped
crying, quieted my body and mind, and all of a sudden as if I
was being directed, I leapt up, ran into the kitchen and opened
up one of the cabinets by the floor, to the right of the stove.
I felt around and couldn't believe it! Motors was just sitting
in the cabinet. I picked him up and kissed him all over, so
happy that he was all right. Then I started to think about what
had just taken place. I had no idea why I went to the kitchen
and opened that one cabinet. There must have been at least
ten different cabinets that I could have opened. But I didn't
open the others. I opened the one he was in. Amazing...or
was it? I never understood it, but I always knew we had this
deep and special connection.

About a year later, I moved into a large renovated barn,
and within a week Bucky disappeared. I let him out early one

morning and he never returned. I was devastated! Bucky had been with me since he was a five-pound puppy. I just expected him to always be there. My friends and I looked everywhere, called all the local vets, had it announced on our local radio station, and had tons of people searching. But despite all our efforts, he never turned up. I never found out what happened to him.

I was overcome with waves of grief for the loss of my best friend. His loss affected Motors, too, and quite severely. He actually seemed to go through a period of depression, just lying around acting lethargic and crying for what seemed like no apparent reason. There was a reason; his big brother was gone.

From that point on, Motors hardly ever went out. When he did, he acted very cautious and scared. He'd smell around a little and then come running back in the house. His big brother wasn't around to watch and protect him. He really missed Bucky.

Eighteen months later, my new partner, Hillary, her five-year-old son, Jory, and I bought our own home and moved in together. The Motor Man was now 13 and going strong. He loved the new house because it had an indoor balcony that made his meows sound more like a mountain lion's roar. He also got to sit in the sun on an upstairs' deck that was totally safe. He had long ago given up hunting for little critters and actually would hang out in Jory's room, listening to the hamster jump around and make noise. Maybe, just maybe, he missed having a friend.

Maybe he did miss having Bucky around or another cat to play with, but he knew he always had my lap and sought it out all the time. It was warm and safe, was often found in the sun, and it had the bonus of loving hands that would always stroke and massage him. It was fascinating how he sought me out. Wherever I was in the house, sooner or later I would find Motors purring softly in my lap. Sometimes he would aggressively seek out my lap, deflecting my rejections and defiantly refusing to be denied. But he could be quite subtle, too. There were plenty of times I found him curled up purring between my crossed legs, having no recollection of how he got there. I guess my warm lap became a safe haven for him. For me, it was second nature to have him close in that special way. Our bonds kept growing.

For the next six years, we all lived comfortably and enjoyed family life. In '85, we got a new dog which Motors promptly trained. He used the fool proof "bloody nose" method he perfected with Bucky so many years ago. Motor Man began to have a consistent desire to be warm, especially in the winter months. His little body was not putting out enough heat so he figured out a way to stay warm. He would scout out where the blankets were kept and burrow until he was under the covers. Most annoying to me and Hilly was his habit of burrowing under our covers at three in the morning. This was apparently his all-time favorite spot. Once again his persistent nature took over. I remember evenings when we would toss him out of bed at least a half a dozen times only to wake up in the morning with him purring under the covers between us.

There were nights we'd come home and Motors would be missing. We knew he was sleeping somewhere under some blanket. We'd never know which room or which blanket, but eventually a soft meow or a startled cat roar would inform us of his whereabouts. Loud roars would come when someone would sit on him. You would just never know. Eventually, we got to the point where we had to feel for bumps whenever we sat down. Hilly used to take pictures of him that way. She'd wait with the camera, focused right on the bump, and I would pull the cover off. Hilly would catch him with that groggy, spaced out look on his face. Precious Fatto!

Motors was such a constant in my life that one part of me really believed he would never die. In fact, his eternal existence was a key factor in my belief in immortality. As long as the Motor Man was alive, nobody could convince me that physical immortality was not a possibility. I used to celebrate his birthdays by getting him shrimp to eat. Somewhere around his fifteenth or sixteenth birthday we had to start breaking up the shrimp into small pieces because he had lost all but four teeth and he couldn't chew very well. I also noticed he was getting lighter. He did not look like a Fat Cat anymore.

In March 1990, Motors turned 19. He was still a spunky, purring, powerful and persistent little prince of a cat. His coat was smooth and shiny, but he had shrunk into an old, elegant friend. His breath smelled, his muscles were atrophying and his bones had lost their solidness. He slept all the time but still he'd seek me out and lick my nose and purr and curl up in my lap like always. Yes, he was finally showing his age. That summer, he gradually stopped eating. At first I thought he was fed up with the brand of food we gave him, but after trying different kinds, we understood. It was very difficult for me to believe he was really dying.

In early August, the Motor Man started to leave. He just refused any food and he began to pee in our bedroom. One night I woke up to find him sleeping at the foot of the bed. Surrounding him was a wet spot. He had lost control of his bladder and I felt horrible. I knew what was happening, but I didn't want to accept it. We borrowed a friend's old dog crate and set up a real cozy little hospice home for him. We put a heating pad on the bottom to keep him warm and on top of that we placed a couple of towels. At night we would close the door so he couldn't wander around. It hurt so much to lock him in. Ever since Albuquerque I had given him all the freedom he wanted, but we couldn't anymore. Sadly, and to my surprise, he didn't seem to mind. He would always curl up and go to sleep. We'd put him in the crate during the day, but we'd leave the door open so he could still move around if he wanted to. Then he started doing weird things. We'd find him downstairs at the door waiting, just waiting to go. One afternoon we let him out in the yard and he started walking

toward the woods. Hilly followed to see where he would go.
She came back with him in her hands. She said, "He was just
going," as if he was being called.

Animals are so connected in those ways. They know
when it's time and they don't resist like people. I cried all the
time now and each day got worse. Motors still wanted to be
in my lap and he'd look for me. If I was on the bed, he would
try to jump up, but he didn't have any strength left. He would
hit the bed about halfway up. Once during that last week, I
was sitting on the floor with my legs crossed. Motor Man
came over and tried unsuccessfully to climb into my lap. I
grabbed him as he fell backwards and placed him gently in
my lap. He fell asleep while purring. He still loved me and
knew where home was. Motors waited for Jory to come home
from camp and then he took his last breath at about 6:30 A.M.
on Saturday, August 25. I had gone to a weekend workshop
the day before, thinking he would hold on until I came back.
I refused to realize how little time he had left. I knew nothing
about death and I think I had run away from looking at what
I didn't want to see. I'd always run from things I didn't want
to see, but never did I regret it as much as this time. I called
Hilly at seven that morning. She told me he had just died. I
was a wreck. My baby had died. I hated myself for not being
with him when he left, but I was fortunate to be with so many
loving, understanding people.

Hilly picked me up and we drove back home, both of us
crying all the way. When I got home I spent a few minutes
with his dead body, but it had little effect on me. His spirit
had moved on. This was not the essence of Motors. I
changed into some old clothes and got a shovel and dug a
little grave across our bridge on the other side of the pond.
Jory and Hilly did their share of digging until the little burial
spot was ready. Then I carried the already- hardening body
outside. Hilly wrapped him in a cloth she had from Binares,
a city in India where they cremate the dead. It was fitting. I
placed him in the hole. With tears rolling down my cheeks,

I methodically covered him with the moist, clay-like dirt. Jory placed a very special stone on the spot; a stone with a big "M" etched on it. Hilly gathered some wild flowers and placed them by the gravestone, and we all said goodby. It was very sad, but at the same time it was also very beautiful. I was so proud of my family. They were just great and I'll never forget how we all joined together out of love and respect for Motors.

I swam in the pond that afternoon and felt Motors watching me. His presence was strong and seemed to be everywhere. After the swim, feeling exhausted from the whole experience, I crawled into bed and fell into a deep sleep. Then I drifted into a lighter sleep and became aware that I had been dreaming. I was lying there, observing my dream, when Motors walked over to my face and licked my nose. The instant his tongue touched my nose, my body experienced a jolt of electrical energy. I rolled over and leapt off the bed from the shock. For a few seconds I remained on the floor, eyes wide open and heart pumping, trying to understand what had just happened. The only thing that made sense was that Motors had crossed over to the other side and wanted to make contact with me one last time, letting me know he was fine and thanking me for the love we shared.

During the next few days, I visited his grave constantly and grieved like I had never grieved before. I fell silent there many times, just being near the warm, secluded area where my friend of so many years was now buried. This land became sacred to me and I felt a growing commitment to this little acre and a half of very special ground. The spirit of Motor Man would always be here.

I also noticed over the next few weeks I had little tolerance for people who were not sincere and serious about doing their best to live well. Life was too precious to be screwing around and letting it slip by. Death was in my consciousness. I learned from Motors' death just how special the gift of life really is. I can't be with people anymore who don't appreciate what it means to be alive.

My adjustment to losing Motor Man was slow and painful. Motors was everywhere in the house. I couldn't go anywhere and not think of him. The downstairs bathroom didn't have his litter box, his food bowl was no longer on the washing machine. But whenever I walked into that bathroom, I automatically stayed to the left so I wouldn't bump into the kitty litter. I can still visualize the bowl of food on the washing machine. Whenever I felt a bump in the bed, I thought of my kitty cat and for weeks I sat down cautiously, automatically worrying about sitting on him. I knew he was dead, but all my actions that had considered him were slow to change. So often we heard sounds that reminded us of Motors moving around the house. We all still wanted him around and we all missed him very much.

When I was eight years old I was visited by four benign, loving spirits. I felt cared for by them and knew things would be all right because they were watching out for me. Years later I realized that these benign, loving spirits were my guardian angels and some weeks after Motors died, I had the revelation that Motors just might have been one of those guardian angels.

Motors lived a wonderful, long, and beautiful life. He lived and died with grace and elegance. We all loved him in our own ways and said goodby that last week in August. He had a beautiful burial with an outpouring of honest love and affection.

Thanks, Motor Man, for all the adventures we shared together and thanks for teaching me so much about giving and receiving love. Thanks for wanting and needing me as much as I wanted and needed you. We were great friends and had a wonderful and long friendship. My sweet kitty cat. I miss you so much.

Marty Klein is a Re-evaluation Counselor and leads workshops on Healthy Relationships and the Liberation of Men. He has also written *Blind Sighted,* a book about one man's journey from sight to insight, which is an autobiography of his struggles and adventures in learning to be an aware, compassionate and responsible man as he lost his eyesight.

Chapter Four

"He often came and stood outside my door
And gazed at me with puzzled wondering eyes,
Like those of humankind by grief made wise-
Who feel that life has little left in store."
- Margaret E. Bruner

My Time Of Need -My Friend Indeed
1939 Nazi-Occupied France

By
Mia LeComte

One day about six in the evening, I came home from one of several jobs I held at the time. I had a small apartment in a little house with a front garden in Fabron, a suburb of Nice. There in front of the door lay a beautiful, sandy-brown Airedale terrier. As I opened the door, he jumped up to lick my hands. When I went into the house, he snuck in behind me. And when I went into the kitchen, the dog followed. I could see he was very hungry. I shared the little food I had and then pushed him out the door, feeling certain such a beautiful dog must belong to somebody.

When I woke the next morning, there again was the dog in front of the house. I gave him a meager breakfast and then he and I both left. It was a beautiful, cloudless autumn day. I wasn't worried about Chiene, as I called the dog. I thought he would go home to his owners during the night or stay outside since it was warm and the weather couldn't hurt him.

I wondered who his owners were. He was an expensive dog and I assumed he had wealthy owners. Perhaps he belonged to an American who had left when the Nazis occupied France, thinking someone would care for him.

Then the weather turned cold and it started to rain. I didn't have the heart to put him outside. At first, I let him sleep in the little living room. Chiene and I became closer and closer. My friends warned me that I was "stealing" a valuable dog, but after two or three weeks, they realized that either he had no owner or something had happened to them. Every morning when I left the house, Chiene went too, and at 1:30 when I returned for my midday meal, there was Chiene again, waiting for food. I discovered that on good days, he walked on the Promenade des Anglais, all the way from Fabron to Nice. Even when it rained my friends would sometimes see him take shelter under a bench. By now, all my friends knew him. They called him Mia's Chiene, the dog who walked elegantly on the Promenade des Anglais.

Most afternoons he stayed home and slept on the couch. After several months, he got used to sleeping in my bedroom. At that time, I had a very low bed, just a mattress on some boards. At first, he would sleep on the floor, but in time he put his head on my pillow right next to my head. It was very comforting to me when I woke in the morning to look into his beautiful, soulful eyes. My husband had just left me. I had loved him very much. He, too, had big brown soulful eyes.

In 1940, it seemed that everyone had become insane. Three weeks after Hitler invaded Czechoslovakia, my husband and I fled Prague. I had just become successful as a painter. The Museum of Modern Art had purchased one of my paintings and well-known collectors were buying my work. But here in Nice, I had to exchange my drawings for food. I had lost everything, but now I had Chiene.

It was the winter of 1939 to 1940. The war progressed and there was less and less to eat. Most of the food I obtained was in exchange for drawings I made on weekends, as I walked in the hills behind Nice. My friends thought I was crazy to share my food with Chiene. I was becoming thinner and thinner while Chiene was getting fat. They thought I should give Chiene away, but I knew I couldn't live without him.

Then one beautiful winter day, I got up early in the morning and went up into the hills to sketch. I came back with many drawings and went immediately to the market in the hope of getting some good food. I found a small piece of meat, a little of this and a little of that. One of the farmer's wives was especially enthusiastic. She took one drawing and whispered in my ear that she would give me something very special. She reached under the cupboard for a little package, a "c'est beure", butter--a whole pound of it! Due to the shortage, there had been no butter for months. I could hardly wait to get home to make myself tea and eat bread with butter.

When I arrived home, I put the butter on the kitchen table and went into the bedroom to change my clothes. Chiene was lying quietly on the kitchen floor. I hadn't gone longer than five minutes before I returned to the kitchen to find Chiene stretched halfway over the table, licking the last bit of butter. Not one little piece was left. I sat down on the floor and cried. He knew he had done something wrong. When he saw me sitting on the floor crying, he came over, put his paws on my shoulder and licked my face as if to ask my forgiveness. I didn't punish him. He must have been just as hungry as I was. That night he slept in my bedroom next to my bed and put his head on my pillow.

The next day, I told a friend what had happened. He said that I shouldn't keep Chiene any longer. "You will both starve to death," my friend said. "What if Italy declares war? You can't drag Chiene behind you. You have to take him to the army to be their mascot."

My friend was right. Two weeks later, Italy declared war on France. All my friends fled to the west. I couldn't because I had no money, my Czech passport was invalid, and I had lost all of my jobs.

The following day, I took a bus into the hills, about 50 miles from Fabron, where there was an army camp. Chiene was sitting at my feet, his paws on my lap. I think he knew I was going to abandon him. I got out of the bus holding Chiene on a rope. Instantly, I was surrounded by young soldiers. There was another dog there, a mongrel, but they wanted Chiene, too. There was a wonderful smell of warm food in the air. Chiene and the little mongrel became friends right away.

I took the next bus back to Nice. It was only when night came that I felt the loss of Chiene. I was now alone in the morning. No soulful eyes looked back at me. Perhaps Chiene missed me, too. Perhaps he was having fun with the little mongrel. When evening came, I felt completely alone and filled with guilt. Maybe I should not have given Chiene to the soldiers. Maybe I could have managed somehow.

Mia LeComte is an internationally known artist and writer. Her story of her escape from Hitler was published by Macmillan in 1941, "The Artist from Prague" in the book *We Escaped*. Mia's book, *Dream of Prague*, published in 1987 was a best seller in the Berkshires and is to soon be published in Prague. She is now living in The Berkshires in Massachusetts with her husband.

Chapter Five

Gray Eyes

It was April when you came the first time to me,
And my first look into your eyes
Was like my first look at the sea.
We have been together for four Aprils now,
Watching over the greens on the swaying willow bough;
Yet whenever I turn,
To your gray eyes over me,
It is as though I looked
For the first time at the sea.
- Sara Teasdale

Dolphin Time

By
Susan Jones

"Life is what happens while you're making other plans," says the magnet I gave my sister years ago, sort of as a joke because she is so organized and draws great comfort from a day well planned. Nothing's wrong with that. It's her path. I've often envied her, just a little, for her controlled, planned, orderly existence, while the rest of me cringes at the trap of it. My life has been messier, a more fluid affair. Details like food shopping, routine meal gathering and preparation, house cleaning; the general attends of daily life, like going to the post office or getting gas. These I've never quite gotten right and regard them as sticky impositions on my time. And I've wanted to get it right--whatever "it" and "right" are.

Life is about finding out what I must do and pursuing it passionately. You can't plan for passion, but you can be open to it and go where it leads. For example, you didn't plan to be passionate about animals. It either happens or it doesn't. It happened for me.

When I was a little girl, I led the neighborhood kids on the mile-long trek into town, shoe box in hand, to the crazy old bird lady's house. We were all afraid of this old, wrinkled bird lady. No one would come with me down the long shadowy driveway behind the scary, dark, old house she lived in. Everywhere there were trees that blocked out the light and made the air smell damp and green. But I found the bird lady was neither nice nor scary. She was just herself, and she always took the shoe boxes with the injured or very young birds we found, shoe boxes lined with grass and dandelions and paper towels and lots of bird-tempting foods. She would take these birds and help them to health or be with them as they died.

We kids never found out who lived or died. We just took our findings gently to her and she always accepted them. We probably went only three or four times over the course of that childhood awakening, but we went as a wide-eyed, rag tag group, filled with hope and wonder. Our journeys there were like parades. It was a most impressionable time. And so it began. My love and appreciation for animals, my concern for their well-being has since become my life's theme. Sadly, I didn't plan for this early in life. I was still busy trying to get "it" "right".

After college where I studied, among other things, people as social animals, I graduated and couldn't find a job. I signed up for seminary studies that I couldn't finish. I then went to work for the phone company and hated it enough to stop. I finally found my way back to the local animal shelter where I had volunteered through high school and became the shelter's manager. All the things we put in our way to keep us from where we must go.

While working at the shelter, I was often reminded of that wonderful wide-eyed parade-like feeling of my little girl days with that interface of caring, hoping, and doing. I met many animals and became, for a little while at least, a part of their lives. It was then and still remains in my heart a landscape of miracles yet uncharted. Every day exploded or unfolded on its own. There were no plans to help us through the day. Guidelines, yes, but it was more like being on the front lines of war or compassion. The unending and unwanted would crowd our shelter and we'd have to deal. It was the hardest job I ever had, and the best.

I met Dillinger along the way, an important dog who taught me what I could and could not do to help animals. Dillinger was a damaged and dangerous dog who'd been quarantined for ten days because he had bitten people. He allowed no one but myself to become involved in his return from the hellish life he had lived up until his shelter confinement. I was able to be part of his transformation into a gentler animal. He did the work. I just helped smooth the way as best I could.

But ten days wasn't long enough to effect change. His owners didn't want him back, there was no place and no more time for him, and so he was destroyed.

The last ten days of his life and his death, which I felt so powerless to prevent, galvanized my heart and mind for continued work with animals. Time with Dillinger ripened my passion for work that can often be crushingly cruel--the stuff of burnout. Cruelty and suffering are everywhere, inside us all and behind the building next door. But Dillinger showed me that can change. I can be in place to offer support, to smooth the way, to assist in regained health or gentle dying. Time with my "angel" named Dillinger showed me how simple and far-reaching a plan for animal rehabilitation can be. Dillinger guided me to my place in that plan. Time spent with a dolphin "angel" showed me how much a part of the plan I am, in ways I didn't realize.

Bats, birds, cats, dogs, rabbits, horses, snakes, and more found refuge in the shelter where I worked--but never a dolphin. Ironic that I found a kind of rehabilitation and shelter from a dolphin who literally saved my life, memories of which give me back my life whenever I recall my Dolphin Time.

We all get "low" but during the hot, sad summer of 1990, I bottomed out. I had seen and been a part of many miracles that occurred between humans and animals, some of them real life-altering changes. But I was so hurt and broken by a marriage I couldn't get "right", I didn't even realize I needed a miracle. I just wanted out, away, an end. As I waded out into the Atlantic Ocean from the Jersey shore, I felt the weight of my life leave me through the salty run of tears. I was 33 years old and hated my life. I was ready to swim to Portugal and beyond. I always felt connected to the ocean, and on that aching early dawn, I was surprised anew at the welcome I felt as the ocean reached out to collect me.

I felt ready and hoped I had the guts to be ready. I had started a committed endurance swim program almost a year earlier because I wanted to enjoy ocean swims more. My family had a summer home on Martha's Vineyard and I always wanted to swim the mile-long stretch of ocean that curved gently between the cliffs at the point and our place. I had finally reached my goal earlier that summer, to my amazement and pleasure. Swimming had become a tonic for my soul. What better way to leave this life than to swim into Neptune's embrace?

My husband's family had a place on the New Jersey shore and we were visiting that week. I felt I had reached the end of myself as I stood at dawn on that empty beach. I was very alone. Would this be a swim or the end?

I was crying loud, heavy sobs into the sea as I felt my way through the water. I remember how muffled my cries sounded under water, different than all those times under a pillow, more interesting, more alive somehow. My ten-year marriage had veered away from those hopes and plans of the happily-ever-after one longs to believe in. That was the summer my husband had to come to terms with my unwavering decision not to bring a child into our destructive relationship. Such a loss of possibilities and hope, of investing in the future only served us more cruelly, each in our own prison and our own destructive dance. So much ended that year, even though it would take four more years to say our last good-byes. It was with a heavy stone-like heart that I went into the sea, certain that where its weight would take me would be better than the life I would leave behind.

I was preoccupied with all the thick, sluggish numbness that comes with such a reckoning, when I first felt him, a gentle nudge against my right thigh. It was a very soft, warm touch, smooth and familiar, not like someone's hand poking, more like a hip pressing into me to get my attention. It did. I was surprised without feeling afraid. I looked about, wondering if someone else was near, even though I hadn't noticed anyone. Then a whitish-gray roundness came up through the water beside me and moved like a ball through the water a few feet in front of me, paralleling the shore. A head! But of what? I was astonished! In an instant, I realized with great relief that it wasn't a shark. I was terrified of sharks, even the remotest possibility of sharks, which made it so amazing that I didn't feel fear at that encounter. No, it was a dolphin! A friendly, round, smooth, soft dolphin! Ever since the television show "Flipper", I loved those curious, gregarious, trustworthy animals and had secretly hoped to swim with one or ride or play with one somehow. But I knew only people like Jacques Cousteau, movie stars, or really rich people could afford to pay to be shipped out to dolphin playgrounds off some exotic port. Only they could be lucky enough to have such an experience. And there I was, seemingly at the end of my life, off the inelegant, unexotic

Jersey shore, swimming with a dolphin! What a mix! I was riveted by this animal! He swam a bit ahead and then doubled back to coax me along. We were playing and swimming. I could barely believe it then, and as I write this all these years since, I see how important it is to remember my Dolphin Time clearly and with all my heart.

I felt like an inhalation, all incoming breath and energy. Then I was swimming with all my might, racing, trying to keep up with him. I was sobbing still, but incredible blasts of energy came over the tears. Shouts and laughter, everything forward as I swam after my ancient friend. I say "ancient" because I felt I was calling, "Hey, wait up! I'm coming!", as though I'd done this many times before. How could I feel so thrilled? How could I even feel? I was at an all-time low in my life and here I was cavorting with a dolphin!

A strange confusion took hold of my soul, interrupting and shifting me. I thought about what I was doing and started to slow down. When I lifted my head out of the water, the first thing I saw was my husband. More confusion. What was he doing here? Why had he bothered to come to the beach so early and in a swim suit? Was he going to swim with me? Oh, go away, I thought. But does he care about me? Why do we keep hurting each other? The only way for us to stop is for me to stop it, I thought. He'll see I'm trying to free us, but maybe we should swim together, with the dolphin, one last time.

My churning thoughts and the shock of seeing him clicked in and out of my consciousness as he ran up the beach, waving his arms furiously, as he shouted at me. I couldn't understand him at first. I pointed toward the dolphin and waved for him to join us. Finally his words took shape in my ears, "GET OUT! GET OUT! THEY CAN KILL YOU! THEY CAN KILL YOU." I looked around and felt and saw all at the same time. The water was alive with dolphins! Everywhere dolphins! As I look back on that startling time, I am reminded of minnows I have watched from docks as they crowd and churn the water in fast, fearful dartings when interrupted from their military-like formations, bodies slipping and slapping in their over-filled momentarily disorganized "schools". Dolphins are more dignified than minnows. They travel in "pods" rather than schools. An orderliness is inferred in the very term "pod", as in "peas in a pod." Dolphins are muscle and air in the water. They are graceful. They don't dart, they dance. They like to touch and rub and when I was among them, I felt like a slipping, slapping nervous minnow who was in the wrong class. "My" dolphin, indistinguishable from this crowd, had seemed gentle and playful, but all the others kept swishing past me, holding their powerful pattern as I dizzily looked about, turning and bobbing in their wake, looking for "my" friend. I half expected Charlie Tuna to pop up and say "Relax. These are dolphins, not fishermen", but the rest of me bought into the terror in my husband's voice. Maybe he was right. Without "my" dolphin guide, I felt even more confused, afraid, and very vulnerable.

I pulled myself in with a spasm, like a snail being poked. I started to gulp and flail as fear flattened the child-like energy that had propelled me through the water moments before. I thrashed away from the dolphins and swam crazily toward shore. Then I stopped, turned back to them and sobbed, "I'm sorry, I'm sorry. I'm too afraid!"

But why was I afraid? I had felt no fear, just exhilaration, wonder and a primitive delight until my husband's warnings. Hadn't I gone in swimming, thinking I wouldn't come out? So why should I fear these amazing animals? If they wanted to play with me, drown me, or eat me, hadn't I already surrendered? I started back into the sea. I was torn by a fearful hesitancy and an internal sunburst of crazy joy and giddiness. And for the second time, I was astonished when "my" dolphin came for me again and swam with me as we sprinted through the surf to join the others.

I remember feeling my face. It was as if I had hung my head out of a speeding car's window, my mouth wide to catch the wind, my voice distorted but gleeful as the air snatched it from my throat, my eyes wide open then shut, open then shut. All this, but underwater. I know I wore a huge smile that let my teeth feel the rush of salt water through them, then out, in, then out, in exactly the right way for me to breathe. All the while tears, but they had turned from their heaviness to tears of joy and amazement.

Another shift with my mind and heart as I wrestled with fear and fell behind again, not sure of what to do, wanting to go on, to be with them, to play and furious at the fear that literally held me back. My tears came angry and hot again, in confusion and disappointment. The fear kept taking over. It was as though there was a valve in me. Open--go, go and play, be happy. Closed--close up, pull back, stop, be afraid. It was a valve that resembled a minnow's mouth--open, closed, open, closed. One moment I was buoyant and swimming, and the next I was frozen and sinking like a lead weight. What a metaphor! What a link up between my body and mind. Minnow me.

That wonderful dolphin found me again, for the last time, and tried to coax and guide me on. In fear I thrashed away from him, a minnow out of school, while sobbing for him to understand, I was too afraid. "I can't! I can't!" I chanted like a plea, begging him to come again someday, another time. Couldn't there be another Dolphin Time?

The dolphin waited for me. He swam back and forth between me and the distancing pod. I was on my knees in the slight surf, doubled over in frustration and disappointment, when, miraculously, as if choreographed, a single whale swam up to the end of the pod and they all swam off in a majestic, rhythmic formation. My dolphin friend finally joined them and left me. It was over. It had taken no more than ten minutes, yet it was like a moment and forever with each beat of my heart.

I had stayed behind. I had been invited, but I had stayed behind. I was stunned and shaken and so disappointed in myself, yet so pleased that I had even had those few minutes with them. I felt recharged with life and the dolphins' wondrous sense of play. It was as though someone had been listening to me, for me, and they had come to comfort and remind me. Connecting with them made me feel alive and able to keep on, to see what was to come. I had not planned a moment of that encounter, and yet it had so altered me, to feel I mattered on a level I didn't even know existed.

For a long time, I let the anger, disappointment, frustration and confusion I felt during that miraculous experience cloud my part in it. Why couldn't I have done it? Why couldn't I have chosen to swim and go with them? Stupid, unable even to kill myself "right".

I see more clearly with each remembrance of my Dolphin Time, what a true angel was sent to me that day, when I was most broken and unable to help myself. That dolphin broke through my brokenness and let me live.

I was given more time than dear Dillinger, but I found a similar inner resolve, as had he, to go on and be gentle with myself. The dolphin was generous and patient with me. I am grateful to him and to the power that moves us all, to have been given an experience of a lifetime which, upon each reflection, incorporates me into a web of living far greater than I know.

I shall call upon my Dolphin Time for the rest of my life. It was not an isolated incident that happened to keep me from a long, early swim. My Dolphin Time interrupts me from my darkness and reminds me that there is more. I remember the fearful frozenness and the exultant openness, and I swim on.

"Life is what happens while you're making other plans."

Susan Jones has been an animal shelter manager in New Jersey and an animal control officer in Massachusetts. Even though all her jobs have not been animal related, she always relates her work to animals. In 1990, while working in a book store in northeastern Connecticut, she founded a non-profit, tax exempt animal adoption and rescue service, A.N.O.N. (Animal Neutering for Orphans and the Neglected) which still operates from the store and from various volunteers' hearts and homes. She currently resides in Massachusetts with her husband and a large animal family.

Chapter Six

The Horse

Hast thou given the horse strength?
Hast thou clothed his neck with thunder?
Canst thou make him afraid as a grasshopper?
The glory of his nostrils is terrible.
He paweth in the valley and rejoiceth in his strength:
He goeth to meet the armed men;
He mocketh at fear and is not affrighted,
Neither turneth he back from the sword.
The quiver rattleth against him,
The glittering spear and the shield--
He swalloweth the ground with fierceness and rage,
Neither believeth he that it is the sound of the trumpet--
He saith among the trumpets, "Ha! ha!"
And he smelleth the battle afar off,
The thunder of the captains and the shouting.
- The Bible: Job

The Rescuer

By
Kate Kennedy

My name is Kate and I have been involved with horses much of my life. All of them have been special to me but none quite as special as Hassan.

I grew up with alcoholic parents who had a great deal of trouble expressing love. As a result they fought constantly. At the age of three, I was a victim of repeated and violent sexual abuse from outside the family. This abuse was not recognized by my family and I was made to believe the abuse was something I deserved. I spent the next thirty years in constant fear of what would happen next.

I do not believe I would have had the strength or desire to survive childhood were it not for my connection to our animals who were always there for me with their love.

As an adult, I grew tired of waking every morning scared to death of what the day would bring. I sought help through counseling for childhood sexual abuse and made great strides toward creating a positive new life. I became certified as an equine trigger point myotherapist to help horses overcome injuries, pain and physical imbalances.

I first met Hassan shortly after receiving that certification. I sought horses to practice on who needed my services but whose owner's couldn't afford it. Payment was optional, a testimonial that my work had been beneficial.

Hassan was then twenty-one-years old, which meant he was getting on in horse years. His body was a deep dark brown with black legs, ears, tail and mane. He had a perfect white star on his forehead and soulful brown eyes which at the time exhibited worry and pain, yet had a spark of playfulness. "San," as we called him, had great stiffness and discomfort in much of his body but especially his back and hind legs. Muscle therapy was helping him but not to the extent I had hoped. I encouraged his owner to seek veterinary advice, which she did. She was told he was just an old horse and it was never pursued any further.

One morning when the barn was particularly quiet and the horses were contentedly munching on their hay, I slipped into San's stall to say hello and see how he was doing. He was always happy to see me and didn't mind as my hands explored his body while he ate. There are times when body work creates a synchronization between the two parties, when a different or higher level of communication occurs. No words are spoken and no analytical mind games played.

There is a heightened sensory awareness and a trust within and between both parties to follow their instincts.   In retrospect, that morning changed the direction of my life.

As my hands moved over San's body, I felt that synchronization occur. Something told me to draw my hands away from his body and simply move them along several inches away. As I did this, I felt resistance in the air, known as an "energy field", and continued to flow my hands through this energy. I felt and saw the tension in his body start to leave. San looked back at me and in my mind, I heard him say, "It's about time!" He let out a great sigh of relief and went back to eating his hay.

The next day a woman at the barn said to me, "I don't know what you did to San yesterday, but he's better than I've ever seen him." Delighted and dumbfounded by her remark, I continued to find quiet moments in the barn to work undisturbed on San's energy. I felt pretty strange about what I had done and didn't need a witness to tell me I had gone off the deep end. I was doing a good enough job of that all by myself. I was so drawn to this new awareness of mine that I immediately sought out books written about "energy work" and started reading.

At the same time, my mother was diagnosed with rapidly progressive throat cancer and had been seriously ill for months. Pain is a big factor in cancer patients as well as fear, and my mother was no exception. I told my mother about San and the energy work I had done. I asked if she wanted me to try it on her. She did and as I worked on her, I again saw the tension start to release. Through the energy work, I felt a love and connection with my mother that I had no conscious memory of ever feeling before As my mother's illness progressed and winter settled in, San moved to another barn and I lost touch with him.

I continued to learn about energy work from a registered nurse who practiced and taught Therapeutic Touch. In the last few weeks of my mother's life, we continued with the energy work. It was obvious that my mother's spirit was spending less time in her body. As difficult as this was for me and my family, it was also a healing time. We were able to let down our guard to feel and express our true emotions.

My mother was in the hospital and at a point near comatose. She had not opened her eyes or communicated with us for more than a day. After practicing some energy work on her, she had a peaceful expression on her face, but I knew she wasn't really there. I sat in a chair and closed my eyes. A few seconds later, I felt myself become weightless and was seemingly transported to a beautiful place of brilliant light, surrounded by a profound sense of love. I felt my mother's presence next to me and knew this was where she would be going. The sensation was so beautiful that I didn't want to leave but knew I had to. When I opened my eyes, I felt surrounded by love. I knew my mother was going to a beautiful place full of love. Before leaving the room, I walked over to my mother and held her hand to say good bye. To my surprise, she opened her eyes. With a sparkling smile I hadn't seen in a long time, she winked at me. "Yes, Kate," she seemed to say, "we were there together. It is a beautiful place and I will be all right." My mother died three days later, just before sunrise with the gentle exhale of a breath and that same peaceful expression on her face.

Once again it was time to recreate my life. My mother's illness had been a healing experience for me. It was a time of love and a step toward forgiveness. The energy work had created a shift in my awareness as I opened myself to a deeper understanding of life, both physically and spiritually. My interest in telepathic animal communication was also becoming stronger. Through the energy work, I had begun to send and receive communication. Now I wanted to further develop that ability.

One day I was moving my horse, Wellie, to a private barn and thought about San as a companion for him. I knew from the previous fall that his owner would be glad to find a good home to which San could retire. I contacted her and made arrangements for San to come live with us. I was told he hadn't been well, but if I wanted him, he was mine.

I hadn't seen San in nearly six months. The day I picked him up, I was shocked by his condition. He was laying down in his stall in what looked to be considerable pain, with no desire to get up or even acknowledge my presence. I was scared by the fact that he wouldn't look in my eyes. It was hard to believe how badly he had deteriorated and that no one had done anything to help. My helper and I got San into the trailer and off to his new home.

The following morning I knew that if San was to live, I had to act quickly. So much was wrong with him that I didn't know where to start. His feet were rotting from filth. He was infested with worms. His teeth could not grind food. He was seriously dehydrated and his body would go rigid in pain when he urinated. What concerned me most was his attitude of having given up. While attending to his basic needs, I contacted an animal communicator. I asked her to pinpoint the area of his worst pain and explain to San that I was offering him a loving home for the rest of his life. If he wanted to fight for his life, I would help him all the way. I would not take on this challenge unless I knew he wanted me to and that he was willing to join me in the battle.

The communicator told me to focus on his bladder and, that San was indeed willing to fight for his life. My vet arrived the next day to examine San's bladder. When asked why I wanted the bladder examined, an unusual request from a horse owner, I fumbled around and came up with an answer I can't even remember. The last thing I would admit was that a psychic told me to.

A rectal exam found the bladder wall thick and painful to palpation. San was put on antibiotics in hopes that we were dealing with an infection. Three weeks and several tests later, San was diagnosed with bladder cancer. My vet was obviously uncomfortable as she broke the news.

Unfortunately, she was leaving for vacation the next day. A horse of San's age and condition was a prime candidate for euthanasia. I took the news in stride and felt cautiously optimistic about San's chances. The mass in his bladder had doubled in size since the first ultrasound, but everything else had improved slightly, especially his attitude. Neither he nor I was ready to give up.

My commitment to San and myself was to let him know true love and kindness before he died. I learned from my mother's death that healing does not always mean to continue to live. I did not know whether San would live or die that summer, but I knew he would be sure of one thing: he was worthy of being loved.

Thanks to a variety of alternative therapies, San continued to improve. The homeopathic vet who diagnosed San as "a brittle and despairing horse who was not quite sure there was worth in living" prescribed a remedy that fit San's symptoms well and said San's chances of survival depended on whether he could "learn to laugh." He also sent an article on how to work acupuncture points for different types of cancer. With the help of another vet certified in acupuncture and chiropractic, I was able to do this. The acupuncture and energy work complimented each other. There were many days when San would not allow me to insert the needles until I had first cleared his energy and opened the points with energy. To simply stimulate needle points and stir up dirty energy is like doing a laundry with dirty water. Healing can only work when the energy is clean.

San's nutrition and detoxification were also paramount. One day while I searched for herbal concoctions to help him detoxify, he provided some answers. I watched as San went to pasture and sought flowers and buds from a wild rose bush, then crossed the grass- filled pasture to eat tendrils of wild growing grapes. I was fascinated by this and went home to read more about herbal remedies for farm animals. To my amazement, rose hips and grape vine tendrils, both noted for their antioxidant qualities, were specifically recommended for bladder cancer.

With the approach of winter, San was stronger than he had ever been. I believe all the remedies helped San get well, but without the communication and energy work, he would not have lasted long enough for them to take effect. During these sessions, I asked for the universal source of healing light to flow through me, that I be guided to know how to help. The key to healing work is in understanding that the "universal source of healing light" is known to us simply as love. That is why this work can be so powerful and the healing effects reach all parties involved.

As winter set in and my muscle therapy business slowed down, I focused on practicing telepathic communication with animals. I had taken a summer workshop but hadn't enough time to utilize my skills. When spring arrived, I felt more adept and initiated a conversation with my horse, Wellie, who had mild digestive troubles. Wellie told me that San advised him to mix his hay with grain which would help balance his system. I was amused and asked what else San had taught him. He said San had foretold of his own death within six months. I felt so shocked and scared that I immediately withdrew from the conversation. San looked and seemed to feel so well that I couldn't understand what was happening.

After composing my thoughts, I questioned San about his supposed death and found him to be quite content with his decision, even though I wasn't. He said, "It would be a time of my choosing, maybe in June or July. What better time to die than in the green and warmth of summer when all is right and my body is most comfortable." I knew I needed time to think before continuing the conversation. Last year when San was ill, I was willing to accept whatever was meant to be. He had gotten well and was no longer attached to his illness. So why was he choosing to die now? Was this going to be another profound lesson for me? I was afraid to ask and I let things be.

Three days later, San and Wellie were playing outside, running, rearing and bucking in very slippery footing. I cautioned San and asked that he please be careful not to hurt himself. Since beginning my studies in communicating, I learned the importance of keeping a pad and paper close at hand to record conversations. San's voice was deep and serious. As much as I tried to avoid the "death" conversation, I knew what he was about to say would have something to do with it and that it would be at length. I ran back to the barn to write down what was coming in to me at full force.

At my request that he be careful, San responded: "If I am to enjoy life, I must take chances. I will not live my life in fear."

His statement hit me in the core of my soul. I knew he was speaking to and about me, as well as himself. I felt mesmerized by his words and intensity.

"On days when I feel good, I will enjoy myself. I'll accept the consequences of my actions and relish in the pain and the joy. You cannot live your life in fear. Let go of your past as you tell others to, and you will live a long, joy-filled life. Hold back on life and it will hold back on you. You are what you do. Don't hold back. Go for it! DO it! BE it! SEE it! And yes, FEEL it! As we have time, I will impart as many of my truths to you as I know. Before I go, you will know that I love you and that you love yourself."

This was the lesson I had intended to teach him last summer. Suddenly it was being turned around on me.

"Open your heart to the song of life. Its words are not always beautiful, but its meanings are. The stories behind the words are yours to find out."

San's voice became deeper and sarcastic. I laughed when he said, "Be not afraid or thou shalt be taken and consumed by the fear of life."

All I could think of was Charlton Heston playing Moses in *The Ten Commandments*. His voice then softened, his words landing gently in my mind.

"You don't have to come back and do this life again, Kate. Learn this life's lesson. Do it and move on."

"What lesson?" I asked San.

"To love yourself and life around you," he replied. "Give in to it. Trust it. Be it. Do it. Feel it. You have the power to love. Give it all and you will get it back twofold. This is the cycle. The cycle of love. You get back what you put out."

In the past, I had done healing work with a Kiowa medicine woman named Little Moon, who spoke of our human experience as the realm of illusion and the realm of the spirit as true reality. When I asked San if he would come back to this world, he was surprised that I spoke of illusion and asked where I had heard this. I told him about Little Moon and the following was his response.

"She has much wisdom. Great Knowledge accepts this world as illusion and spirit as reality. Great Knowledge can guide us down the path we've chosen to take. This world of illusion can impart great pain. Knowing it is illusion can ease the choices we have made along the way. You don't always know the right way to go. Great Knowledge is there to guide us and make our path have meaning. Learning about this life of illusion is what Great Knowledge has in mind. It is a folly on his or her part. There is no true pain, only learning and experience. In this reality, sometimes it is hard to accept, especially when the pain feels greater than we can endure. Remember this: We are never given more than we can endure. Even if it takes us from this world of illusion. It is our lesson. Death, whether abrupt, painful or peaceful, is part of the story and part of what we were meant to be or do."

He hesitated and then said, "You tire from this information. I will teach you about death before I go. You will always know love throughout."

San was right, I was exhausted. The power of his words had blown me away. As much work as I had done to get fear out of my life, I realized that with the newness of the energy and telepathic work, fear of the unknown was stealing back into my life. As beautiful as all this newness was, I was still afraid of the unknown, of being different, of being who I really was, and of allowing joy into my life. I felt like my child-self again, always waiting for the other shoe to drop and never believing I was worthy of love or joy. San had re-exposed the wound whose depth had not completely healed. He was there to help me deal with it so that I could move on.

In subsequent conversations, I discovered that San was planning to leave because he thought he had become a burden. My muscle therapy business was booming and I had much less time for my animal friends. When I realized this, I assured San that he was not a burden. I reflected back on everything this horse had taught me since our first meeting two years ago. My muscle therapy technique was honed on him. My energy work was created and initially taught by him. He taught me about the body's innate ability to know what it needs to help itself and recognize that everything of Earth emits an energy. We can recognize these as beneficial or hazardous to our wellness. The incredible experience with my mother would never have happened were it not for San. Through him I came to know the remarkable effects of homeopathy and developed a basic understanding of oriental medicine and chiropractic. More than anything else, this horse had opened my eyes, heart and soul to the universal source of truth and love.

How could I possibly let San think he was a burden? I thanked Hassan, my dear friend, healer and spirit guide, and asked that he stay in my life for as long as it suited him. I did not get an answer from San and did not press for one. When I walked into the barn the next morning, his gleaming face with the perfect white star and sparkling eyes greeted me with a loving hello. He ate his breakfast with vigor and had an unusual spring to his step as I led him out to pasture. I had my answer and we've never talked again about his leaving me.

Another year has passed since these first conversations, and San is still with me. I cherish him now more than ever. I have received so much guidance, love, wisdom and humor from this dear friend that I cannot imagine life without him. He brightens every day with his presence.

As I look back at my original intent to rescue San, I have to ask the question, "Who rescued whom?"

Kate Kennedy is an Equine Trigger Point Myotherapist and energy worker as well as animal communicator. She resides with her husband and various animal friends in the northwest hills of Connecticut.

Chapter Seven

"Your wistful eyes searched each one as he passed.
Stray dog--so lost, so starved and starkly thin,
And yet your gallant hope held to the last
That there would come a heart to take you in."
- Charlotte Mish

Ain't Nothing Better Than
A Coonhound

By
Joan Embree

Even though I loved Elvis Presley with each volatile hormone of my heart-wrenched fourteen-year-old self, I knew the way he denigrated hound dogs as he gyrated in his tuxedo on the Ed Sullivan Show wasn't right. There he was, on the small, round Magnavox screen that rested in its blond, wooden cabinet, crooning with pouted, swollen lips his near-grief that his hound dog was nothing because he never caught a rabbit. Thrusting his hips in distress, he called his dog a liar and said he was no kind of friend. The hound, wearing a top hat and perched high on a stool, looked mournful as Elvis ruthlessly tore his reputation to shreds. Even knowing Elvis was dead wrong about his dog, I admit that I too screamed with hysterical abandon, along with my four girlfriends who sat mesmerized each and every time he tossed his black, glistening hair and sexily sneered. Still, I wondered how that adorable hound made out in life.

I wasn't to meet a hound dog until I was a grown woman living in Washington, D.C. with my husband, Tim, and our two children, Isabelle and Blair, aged four and two. It was in the summer of 1972, when the city was held in a siege of unbearable heat and insect bliss. Locusts crooned their drone-chant day and night, their masses blackening the hazy sky, imbuing leaves and flower petals with big, gaping holes. Black brittle corpses of exoskeletons lay clustered like fallen armies at the base of trees. The city's humidity provoked a sub-army of slugs curled around the rims of teacups left out overnight on patios, their silver slime laying in wondrous, miniature trails.

Isabelle, Blair and I often sought refuge on the cool trails deep in Rockcreek Park. One muggy morning, as we strolled along singing Broadway show tunes, we heard a soft moan above our imperfect voices. We couldn't figure out where the sound was coming from. It was sad and intermittent, and seemed to emanate from several directions. We walked in circles trying to locate it, and finally came to a small mound at the edge of the dirt path, near a Magnolia tree. At first, we didn't know what we were looking at. Gradually, we recognized the mournful, blinking eyes of a dog. His body was rawboned and meager, more bare than covered with fur. He was tied to the tree with a piece of ragged rope, left there to starve to death. What fur he had was clumped and matted with dried, black blood. Isabelle and Blair cried, "Oh, poor thing! Mommy, look at this sad dog!" I remember being struck by his beauty, his onyx jewel of a nose, the sable depth of his sooty-edged eyes, those long velveteen ears. Clearly, this was a hound dog, similar to Elvis's.

Our newfound dog didn't flinch as I scooped him up. He seemed light as a feather that had floated down from heaven and landed gently under a tree for us to find. We went immediately to the animal hospital where a doctor suggested it might be best to put the dog to sleep, considering how far gone the animal was. We wouldn't hear of that. It took only two months to nurse our coonhound back to health. This was not a difficult task. All he needed for a full recovery was lots of love, food and more love. We named him Sam, after Sammy Davis Junior, who could tap dance like no one else.

Not long afterwards, Tim was hired to publish a new magazine in Albany, New York, and so, we packed our bags, shipped our furniture, gathered up our four blue-gray cats and one fine hound and flew Allegheny (better known as Agony) Airlines into Albany Airport. Traveling with so many animals proved to be a harrowing journey. The cat carriers were placed on the revolving luggage belt, with gray paws sticking out of the airholes, scratching frantically in thin air. I felt horrified that some of the cats had almost escaped from the thick, but obviously not thick enough, cardboard carriers. The thought of them lost forever at the airport was appalling. A hideously, long pause ensued in which Sam's carrier did not roll onto the automated belt. When it finally did arrive, the children and I were so overcome with joy at the sight of Sam with his drooping ears, a pathetic and forlorn expression on his face behind the bars of the cage, that we laughed and hooted loudly. A woman standing nearby admonished us severely for what she took to be cruel glee at the sight of our dog's misery. She even threatened to report us to the humane society. But the more she scolded, the more we couldn't stop laughing. Tim, being reserved yet prone to droll humor, told the woman she ought to pity him because he suffered the great misfortune of sharing his bed with twenty-six feet other then his own.

We settled happily into a farmhouse nuzzled deep in gold, far-flung hayfields. The Housatonic River wound around lower meadows dotted with clover and purple thyme, from which rose two enormous, dark green haybarns. Blue, silver-misted Berkshire hills undulated along the horizon like prehistoric beasts. Sam, howling and careening across the landscape, thought he had died and gone to heaven. On full moon, neon-white nights, he'd point his nose up to the sky, emitting soulful, unearthly howls, his long throat vibrating with ululations like a fine instrument. Even the coyotes would join in. To this day, I have not heard a symphony that could top the splendid and spine chilling ones of those nights.

Sometimes, when the wind knocks at my doors, scuttling dead leaves like crabs across an Autumn-stark lawn, moaning as it does behind the shutters, I imagine it also moves the ghost of Sam. It is then that I can see him, leaping over fallen logs in full pursuit of a lumbering woodchuck or a racing rabbit, his hound body lean and stretched as he ran into the darkened depth of trees. My memory's ear hears his howls, his "barking-ups", music destined to break your heart.

I am continually astounded at the presumption and ignorance of people who say only human beings have thoughts and emotions, that the so-called lower forms of animal life function according to instinct. As if instinct itself isn't an elegant form of genius. Sam certainly dispelled this prejudiced notion. Indeed, he was a deep and profound thinker. You could see in his eyes all possible emotions: love, compassion, empathy, fear, sadness, happiness. Sam had great insight with the children and knew about the importance of sharing. For example, Isabelle would lick an ice cream cone, pass it on to Blair to lick, who in turn held it to Sam's salivating mouth. Sam did not, as one might expect, wolf it down. He'd take one polite lick, then turn his face to Isabelle, obviously saying, "Your turn, Belle."

Sam was good at problem solving, too. One afternoon, I was having lunch in our farmhouse with a new friend, thinking this was the civilized thing to do, when, in fact, I would have preferred being out in the fields with Sam and the children. Lunch began to feel everlasting and without end. I'm quite sure that Sam, my man, had decided enough was enough. He skulked unseen into the dining-room and slipped under the table, where he suddenly let forth a blood-curdling howl that caused both myself and my guest to drop our forks and simultaneously rise up from our seats. Having composed herself, the woman dared to peek under the table, whereupon she, in turn, let out a scream so deafening it sent Sam scrambling out from under the table to hightail it back outside. His long, velvety ears flew out like airplane wings and his eyes were wide with terror. I don't suppose he had anticipated so violent a reaction.

The woman stood, her hand delicately at her throat, and said, "Oh, dear, I'm afraid I have to be going. I feel rather ill." I looked under the table and there, neatly placed where her feet had been, was the severed head of a rabbit. The stem of its neck was scarlet and filleted to reveal ligaments, delicate and shiny like thin silver ribbons.

In addition to problem solving, I believe this episode showed that Sam was brilliant enough to understand that one thing can have many meanings. For example, had he laid the poor rabbit's head at my feet, it would have been recognized as a gift, as though he had bestowed me with a kiss. Sam knew I accepted him for who he was; an incorrigible hound with an insatiable need to hunt. Even though I didn't eat meat and I loved bunny rabbits, I didn't begrudge him his needs. I did try to scold him nicely, but it did no good.

And in return for my tolerance, Sam gave me more than I can say. He taught me how to see the beauty of the country, city girl that I was. Together we contemplated thin, winter moons slung like pale slices of eternity. We saw bird's nests made of moss and wool too perfect for art and too cunning for nature. We saw honeybees on white clover in fields of lean hay swaying in summer breezes, immoveable plows in unmown fields, meadows dotted with swells of woodchuck homes, cows staring off into secret places beyond human vision. Sam, Isabelle, Blair and I slept among wild roses mangled into hedgerows, yellow yarrow, buttercups and cinquefoil splattered like abstract art.

One late afternoon, Isabelle and Blair, deciding to be independent and free, took off across the fields on their own. It was the first time I did not know their whereabouts. I raced through the house, calling for them. Then I tore across the fields and ran to the barns. They were nowhere in sight. I ran to the river, fearing the worst. Sam ran on ahead of me, weaving and circling, his nose close to the ground. Suddenly, he took off in the direction of a line of trees separating our property from that of our nearest neighbors, about two acres away. Although I tried to keep up with him, he left me far behind. Not long after, he returned holding the hem of Isabelle's negligee in his mouth, as he pulled her along. Her daily costume at that time was an old negligee of mine, red high-top sneakers and a rhinestone tiara. Blair ran behind them in his emerald green superman cape, the back of it emblazoned with a large, satin "S".

"Where did you two think you were going?" I scolded.

"We didn't think. We knew. We were going over to Harry's," Isabelle said in her usual forthright manner.

"He needed to see my cape," Blair said. Sam blinked at me. I think he was telling me to lighten up.

One late afternoon, a red pick-up truck pulled into our driveway, slowly, as if in a dream. The driver, a young man in overalls, walked stiffly over to where I stood in the garden, knee-high in Swiss chard. The children were on their swings, sailing high into the sky from the thick boughs of ancient maple trees, one tree growing next to the other. The man moved so slowly and bore no expression on his face.

He said, "You own a hound dog?"

"Yes, I do." I said.

"Afraid I have some bad news. You better come with me," he said kindly.

I got into his truck and we drove down to the main road. There was blood everywhere or so it seemed. Off to the side I saw Sam's limp body. Incoherently, I said, "Where's his head? I don't see his head. Maybe this is not my dog." I tried willing it to be the truth, that this could not be Sam. But I knew even before I saw Sam's face, that it was him. I knew by the colors of the crumpled body, the brick red-brown of his shoulder, the soft purple tones of the hollows of his belly, the chocolate-gray edge of his ear caressing the cruel road.

A deep, thick pain wrapped around my chest. It settled there for a very long time. I saw the blood in the road for weeks and months after rain, ice and snow had washed it clean. The winter became interminable. Tim rarely came home. I wanted to be happy again, to run in the fields and play with Blair and Isabelle, but my heart felt dragged down, like a stone or an empty clay vessel. I knew that somehow, if only for the children's sake, I had to wrench myself free of this grief.

Early one evening, I asked the children if they would run in the hay field with me, down to the river's edge. I asked if we could run as fast as possible, until our hearts pounded loudly in our ears. They thought this was a grand idea. We ran and ran, our mouths open and gasping. We tripped and rolled down on top of one another and wrestled on the cold, hard ground. I turned my face up to the blue-black, starlit night and called silently to God, asking him to rid me of my sadness.

A fierce wind came up out of nowhere. The night turned suddenly cold. I saw a shadow move out from behind a mulberry tree. A lean, shepherd-collie loped toward us. Even in the near darkness, I could see his golden coat, because he was surrounded by light. He had an air of confidence about him, as if he was not a stranger. He walked directly up to me and looked deeply into my eyes, gently taking hold of my wrist in his teeth, not hurting me in the slightest. He led me back down to the larger of the green barns. Isabelle and Blair followed along behind us. We climbed the haybale steps up into the barn and sat, the four of us in the wide, flung-open doorway, our faces turned to the river. We sat there quietly, obediently, hearing only the wind in the hills. The wind moaned, orchestrating black limbs of trees to rise up closer to heaven, moving ghosts along. Then we heard Sam. We heard his howls, the full range of them, mellow and mournful and full of music.

"Mommy," said Blair, "Sam is here again, only we can't see him."

"That's okay, Blair," Isabelle said, "at least we know he is home and happy."

"I think Sam told this other dog to move in with us," Blair said.

"Yes, of course he did. He's going to be our new guardian angel," Isabelle said in her usual doubtless manner.

We named our new dog Buford, after Buford Pusser, the sheriff in the movie, *Walking Tall*, who was brave and fearless like no one else.

❀❀❀❀❀❀❀❀

Joan Embree, a cook, writer and Ashtanga Yoga practitioner, lives in The Berkshires of Massachusetts and has the great fortune of sharing her house with three dogs (Mamie, a coonhound, Kara, a Samoyed, and Mr. Brown, an elegant mixed breed) and six cats (Sandra Green, Teddy, Dan, Joshua, Mia and Jeff).

Chapter Eight

"...so I beg that you will not
Defame or desecrate this spot
By ruthless act or idle jeer,
Though but a cat lies buried here."
- Margaret E. Bruner

Kitty

By
A. M. N.

It all began on July 18, 1996. My husband Chris and I were eating breakfast when we saw an orange tabby cat drinking water out of Putzel's outside bowl. Putzel is our indoor-outdoor cat. The visitor was an undernourished stray with dull-looking fur, who appeared only rarely during the next two weeks. Knowing winter would be upon us soon, I felt I had to do something to capture the trust of this skittish creature who had barely an audible meow. I decided I would put out food each night and then befriend him. I would have a vet check him out and finally put him up for adoption. That was the plan.

I named the cat "Kitty", though he was at least a year or two old. At the time, we didn't yet know that he was male. Kitty came almost immediately to eat the nearly two pounds of cat food I left out daily. He would eat it in one fell swoop, around 8:30 at night. Despite the food, Kitty trusted no human and fled when anyone approached.

On the day after Labor Day, Tuesday, September 3rd, I had returned from a day's outing at Mystic Harbor in Connecticut. Due to several tragic car accidents I had witnessed that day, my nerves were frazzled by the time I arrived home. Kitty was waiting for me in his favorite spot, by the large flower border outside the kitchen window. I fed him and then invited him to be friends with me. To do this, I took a non-threatening posture. I sat on the lawn where I completely quieted myself inwardly in order to direct love toward this dear creature. For over half an hour, I sat on the lawn, legs stretched out, leaning backward on my hands and looking at the sky.

I was five feet from Kitty. Then, miracle of miracles, he slithered on his side until he came up to my outstretched legs. He sniffed me, then walked onto my lap where he rolled on his back, allowing me to gently touch his belly. He rolled over and purred, gently kneading me. As he looked up at me, I sensed something very special about him but couldn't quite define it. From then on, Kitty appeared regularly between 4:30 and 8:30 at night for two separate feedings and human love.

I learned on our initial greeting that Kitty was a very unneutered male. I thought it best to get Kitty neutered, tested for feline leukemia, and most importantly, get a rabies shot. After all, Putzel was our cat and I didn't want to endanger his health in any way. I arranged to have him examined by a vet in Connecticut who dealt with strays and feral cats. In time, I succeeded in gaining enough of Kitty's trust to have him enter the cat carrier on his own. However, when I closed the latch, he erupted in panic and fury. Once we got Kitty in the car, he panicked so much that he opened the carrier's latch by himself. It was my worst nightmare. He bounced off the closed car windows in sheer terror. I knew then that this cat treasured his independence and would never be caged by anyone. The minute I let him go, he was my friend again, loving me unconditionally. We never got to the vet in Connecticut.

My next attempt was to have a vet come to the house. A female vet was found who was willing to participate in this plan. The first time she came, Kitty barely allowed her to touch him. He sensed her "authority" which infringed on his sense of independence, and he bolted from my lap and fled into the surrounding woods. The second time the vet arrived, he never showed up. Instead, three tom turkeys came and entertained us. As she was pulling out of the driveway and onto the country road where we live, Kitty climbed out of the crab apple tree and walked over to me. He had been observing us the entire time. I called the vet shortly after. She thought Kitty had been abused and abandoned in the past and it would take more time to establish a trusting relationship with her. Her main concern was to give the cat a rabies shot as protection, not only for Kitty and Putzel, but also me. We devised another plan, but that one never materialized.

Kitty arrived regularly at 4:30 and again around 6:30. Often, he craved much more than food, longing for love and acceptance by a human. He showed this by refusing to eat until he had jumped onto my lap. He longed to be stroked and would purr so loudly that I felt his chest would burst. When he'd had enough, he would then eat dinner, only to return for more human-feline interaction. These nightly rituals not only pleased Kitty, but definitely nourished me. On my fifty-third birthday, he came and wanted lots of love and hugs. That day, he taught me how often we feel we want to be fed physically, when what we really long for is loving nourishment.

The following day, on October 7th, my heart broke in two. Kitty was killed by a car fifteen minutes after I last saw him. He came earlier than usual that night and enjoyed a treat of chicken skin and IAMS ocean fish. He didn't seem to want to leave me so we sat outside for almost forty minutes. Then he jumped away and went to his flower border which was full of daisy mums. Just as he was about to go on his way for the night, I somehow felt a need to take some photographs of him. In the last shot, he was walking by the rhubarb patch and I thought, "He looks like he's walking into the sunset," which, in fact, he was literally doing. He turned and looked at me, asking for more food and stroking. He was indulged and certainly seemed to love it. Chris came home earlier than usual. He saw us and proceeded to sit on the kitchen stoop. Kitty greeted him and walked away.

We got a pallet from a neighbor's dumpster and set the foundation for Kitty's winter home. A friend had loaned me a small outdoor, weatherproof dog house that would be perfect for an outdoor cat like Kitty. The house had lots of straw around it and sat on the pallet in a very protected area. Kitty could be sheltered for the winter if he chose to do so.

I went inside to serve supper which had been cooking all this time. We had just sat down when the doorbell rang. It was our dear friend, Brenda, who was on her way home from work. She had seen a cat lying on the road and thought it was Kitty. It was. He was warm, but dead of head injuries. He had been hit by a vehicle.

Rarely have I ever cried as much for anyone as I did for this furry creature. As darkness fell, I sat by the grape arbor with the physical remains of my friend and contemplated our short but intense friendship while my husband dug a grave in Kitty's border. There were so many reasons why this animal had such an impact on my life. He was not only loving, but lovable. He was innocent, a survivor in a harsh world, a little being who had been abused, abandoned and forlorn, yet had found new meaning in life. That certainly was a lesson for me. We respected each other and, at the end, forgot about agendas and plans. We respected our free spirits and individualities. But perhaps most importantly, Kitty dared to trust and love again, no matter what happened in his past. He taught me that living in the moment was what counted. If he could overcome the hurt and pain from his past, so could I. He loved unconditionally, something I longed for at the time. He didn't care if I was overweight, if I wore denims all the time, if I wore no makeup, or if I was moody. He just accepted me and showed his love, appreciation and complete trust. Because of this, he helped heal me physically, emotionally and spiritually. He was a messenger from the spirit world teaching me these lessons.

Today, I am grateful I had been kinder than usual to Kitty that last evening. I am especially thankful that I looked long and deeply into his beautiful yellow eyes. There was magic in them that I sensed that night, but really experienced on October 7th. They were yellow suns full of love, light, compassion, acceptance, friendship, trust and respect.

The night he departed from the physical world, I dreamt of Kitty. He thanked me for having supported his existence while on earth. I didn't betray him as others felt I should. "Befriend him," they had said, "then take him to the Humane Society in Pittsfield to be euthanized. He is only a stray!" Kitty had a great summer with us, getting food and shelter, lots of love and respect. God bless you, my little free spirit!

Epilogue

On Thursday, October 9th, while drying some fresh basil in our gas oven, I went upstairs to do some desk work in my study. It was cool outside and the windows were closed. During the next few hours, I began to feel nauseous and headachey.

When I went back into the kitchen later that day, I thought I saw an image of Kitty out of the corner of my left eye. He darted by me to stand before the oven and meowed quietly. At first, I dismissed the incident as the result of heartache over his loss. Then the thought occurred that perhaps Kitty was trying to tell me something. I stood in front of the oven wondering what it could be, when I thought I should check the pilot light in the broiler. It had, in fact, blown out. I relit the pilot light, turned off the oven, opened all the windows and doors, and thanked Kitty for alerting me to the danger of carbon monoxide poisoning. Even in death, he was a true friend.

❁❁❁❁❁❁❁❁

A. M. N. lives in the beautiful Berkshires with her husband Chris and cat Putzel. She has created a wildlife habitat, especially for butterflies and ruby-throated hummingbirds. She is an artist, photographer and nature writer.

Chapter Nine

"There appeared a chariot of fire,
and horses of fire, and parted them both asunder;
and Elijah went up by a whirlwind into heaven."
-The Second Book of Kings, II:11

An Angel By My Side

By
Sara Manuel

She pranced off the trailer like an angel, softly stepping down from the heavens and into my life. She was like nothing I had ever seen before. Just her existence mesmerized me. I stood back and watched as the cloudy, dreary day turned into sunshine as streams of beauty poured from her body. Her soft, white coat and mane shone in the non-existent light, drawing me closer. I took her lead and walked beside her, feeling her presence, her head held high like the proud Arabian she was. She always faced life head on and never backed down from anything. Walking along with her, I, too, felt tall and proud. It was then that I felt myself change. I knew from that moment everything was going to be a little different, a little better. And as we walked side by side, I felt our two souls gradually melt into one.

Her name was Ultima II, but we just called her Tima. She was a sixteen hand, pure-bred Arabian horse with licensed papers. She was always referred to as my mother's horse because a good friend of the family gave her to my mother. This made me furious and incredibly jealous. She was mine and always would be. Every night when I went to feed her, I would brush her down, comb out her mane, and just sit and talk to her. We could talk for hours about everything, from world wide issues of war and poverty to the most minuscule and petty problems in my life. She understood every word, much better than any human I've ever met. She was always there whenever I needed something, whether it was someone to talk to and share my pain or joy with, or if I just needed a hug. She was always there. And when I was sad, she would turn her head around and nuzzle me, even if it meant leaving her precious food.

Tima was a proper lady, yet highly spirited and always full of life. She was gentle and comforting while strong, powerful and dominant. She was full of passion and love. She had a knowing look in her eye that would reach out, and you couldn't help but smile.

Tima always befriended everyone. My pony, Peanut, always had a bad attitude. She would nip at you and never listened to anyone. She was, and still is, in desperate need of attention, but she is too proud to let you give it to her. But she was never like that around Tima. They were best friends and would go crazy if they were ever separated. But Tima was more than that. She was like an older sister to Peanut. She gave Peanut the discipline she never received when she was young. So Peanut lost her attitude when she was with Tima. She kept it with me and my family, but with Tima she moved above it.

Even my dad liked Tima. Not that my dad dislikes horses. He doesn't, or any other animal for that matter. It's just that he's very particular about which ones he likes.

Then there was our relationship, mine and Tima's. We weren't only best friends. We were soul mates.

It was the summer of 1995 and it had been about a year and nine months since Tima had arrived. I was in Arizona visiting my aunt. My mom decided she was going to go riding every week with our neighbor, Carol. She had just saddled up

Tima and was beginning to mount her when the saddle slipped. Carol reached through the fence to tighten the girth, but in doing so hit the electric fence, which they had forgotten to turn off. The electricity traveled from the electric socket to the wire, through the wire to Carol, and through Carol to Tima. Tima jumped and my mom fell, breaking her pelvis. She would be in bed for at least a month.

While my mom lay in her hospital bed, the doctors discovered she had an irregular heartbeat that was causing blood clots. The blood clots nearly killed my mom. Tima had saved my mom's life.

But it didn't stop there. Tima probably saved the rest of our lives, too. That summer, my family and I had been planning a vacation to Panama City, Florida, right when the big hurricane hit. Since my mom couldn't move, we didn't go.

On the morning of August 2, 1995, I went down to feed Tima, as usual. She was bright and cheery and eager to get her food just as she always was. I rubbed her head and neck and gave her a kiss on the nose. I went across the street to visit with my neighbor and bring back some food she had prepared for my family. Thirty minutes later, I came back to find Tima lying motionless on the ground.

At first, I rushed to my mother for help, but there was nothing she could do, no comfort she could give. I felt as though I was thrust into a pool of ice cold water. It was too cold to move and too much of a shock to breathe. I looked around in desperation for someone to pull me out, but there was no one there. I was left to drown in my pain. I felt my care-free world crumble around me and fall to the ground as I lost the last of my ignorance and was left to face reality.

Tima died at the young age of eight with no health problems. It was her time to die. Tima came into my life bringing happiness and hope. She saved my family and taught me how to love. And when she was through, she left quickly, peacefully, and painlessly.

I used to cry every night and pray to God that I would wake up and discover it was only a dream. Or, if not, at least I could have died instead of Tima, for her life was worth so much more than mine. But after a while, I realized that it was meant to be, that she has given me a gift more precious than anything I ever received. Maybe now I can give this same gift to someone else. But first, I have to move on. And in order to do that, I must give her something back. So this is for you, Tima.

I will love and remember you forever, Your Soul Mate, Sara Alethea.

Sara Manuel is a 14-year-old dreamer, aspiring actress and animal advocate.

Chapter Ten

Isabella Says:

*Though I can no longer dance before you in a little
cat body
I am dancing for you in the fire of the candle flame
and the sparkling waters of the waterfall.
It's all the same. It's true!
You don't need my body to feel my love and delight.
What you need is to feel this love and delight
in the very depths of the materiality
that causes your seeming pain.
So let this message enliven you
and let me shine through every smile.
Really!
If you 'really' love me find delight in every moment
as I did and I will live through you
Ooo!*
- Cassia Berman

An Initiation from the Catguru

By
Cassia Berman

Over the years, I've written to my friend, Jeri Becker, about my wonderful family of cats. She is allergic to cats, but in the prison where she is a lifer, she watches the other women bond with the wild cats who come to the prison yard. Here, they eagerly offer what little food they can save in grateful exchange for the cats' attention and affection. Jeri is a yogini, who not only describes these women who serve the cats, but can also detect the heart's opening they seem to receive in return. In one of her letters, she coined the phrase 'catguru'. A Satguru, in Sanskrit, is the highest guru, that greatest of all teachers who opens the way for you to absolute truth, love and wisdom, and whom you honor as your personal embodiment of the divine.

Two days after Kuthumi, my almost thirteen-year-old black-and-white tuxedo pussycat sweetheart, companion and playmate, passed out of the physical realm (not a euphemism for death, but a description of how it looked as it happened), I remember our time together and reflect on what I've experienced since. Heavy crying, of course, but also a lightness in the heart, a new strength and energy in myself. This morning it comes to me: Kuthumi has given me a mantra! He was my 'catguru' indeed! A mantra is a phrase or syllable, said silently or aloud, and usually given in a ceremony of transmission that opens and connects you to reality and transforms your consciousness. To hold its initiatory power, it's usually kept as a secret between receiver and transmitter. I suddenly realize 'catgurus', like all in the natural world they're so close to, are constantly saying mantras aloud for all to hear. The only secret is in one's openness to receive.

The mantra Kuthumi gave me is "Waaaaa!" said in a high, enthusiastic, open-throated voice, and almost a shout. "Waaaaa!" is what Kuthumi would say in greeting whenever someone entered the garden gate. He'd stand there expectantly, with his tail held straight up like an exclamation point, or walk back and forth with joyful insistence, until each new person petted him. Petting Kuthumi, who had fur as thick as a plush toy animal, always felt to me more a gift to the petter than a request for his own satisfaction. The word 'darshan', which means to receive the blessing of a holy one's presence, used to come to mind. "Waaaaa!" he would shout and demand you to experience his good nature and love, and give him the wonderful chance to know you. When he was a kitten, I gave him the name of the Ascended Master, Kuthumi, because it had always sounded like a good name for a cat. As Kuthumi grew, he turned out to be a master pussycat, with a special radiant quality of nobility, generosity, wisdom and love in his playfulness and beauty. I've been in love with other cats, but it was only Kuthumi who called this specific language of blessing to my mind.

However, thinking of being initiated into a mantra also brings to mind Isabella, Kuthumi's little sister, who looked like his twin but for her one white eyebrow. (Kuthumi had two sets of varying numbers of long white eyebrows like electric antennae.) Isabella was born in the litter after Kuthumi and of the same mother, my first soul mate, Kate. Gladootchkie, Kuthumi and Isabella used to hang out together, sometimes almost becoming one cat. They would sit parallel to each other and turn their heads or raise their paws to groom in unison. The mantra Isabella gave me was "Olllll!" also said in a high voice. Isabella would constantly sing it as she rubbed with delight against flowers, trees, furniture, anything she could find. Isabella was wise too, but acted really silly. For almost eleven years, she was in a constant frenzy of delight. She died a year and a half ago, and almost tore my heart to pieces doing so. Her parting gift was to tell me that, whenever I experienced the delight she felt every moment in being alive--and which so delighted me to watch--when that delight was 'inside' me, we would be close, and she would be present. Sometimes I find myself saying "Oooooo!" and feel her dance in my heart.

Kuthumi died peacefully after nine months of dealing with failing kidneys and liver. When the other cats needed to go, I had the strong intuition to let them, and never knew if what I did was right. But when Kuthumi got sick, I took him to vets and healers and did everything I could to help him stay. In the last two months he became emaciated. He lost a line of fur along his spine and down to the base of his tail. He frequently had trouble eating and keeping food down, but to the amazement of the vets, he stayed alive and I was committed to helping him. It was dismal for both of us, but there was such love and loyalty between us that I think we both treasured our time together. I know I did. I pretty much stopped living my life to stay home with him. He purred and stayed close to me, his sweet, playful spirit toned down but still shining in his fading body.

Two mornings ago, although at first I didn't want to believe it, my intuition told me this was the end. Despite a new homeopathic and nutritional regimen, he continued to get weaker. This time I knew not to take him to the allopathic vet or try to do any energetic healing on him myself. He died peacefully, gradually getting weaker during the day, stretched out and breathing, with a few light seizures toward the end, as if to help shake him out of his body. It felt like most of what I knew as Kuthumi had left his body many hours before he stopped breathing. With my mind's eye, I could even see his beautiful pussy face, hovering overhead.

It was then I received the mantra--"Waaaaa!" right in my heart. I've been pretty much withdrawn from human company the last few months. It felt as though Kuthumi ordered me out of the house and sent me to the health food store, where despite the late hour, I met several people I knew. "Waaaaa!" I heard inside myself. "Be friendly!" I let myself be open and investigate them with new, more trusting eyes, kind of rubbing against them and letting them rub against me as he would have. "Waaaaa!" and as I let Nancy walk me home and talked about my grief with her and all the others, I really didn't feel alone, even though for the first time in almost twenty years, there were no cats to come home to.

"Waaaaa!" might seem a simple thing, but the most simple spiritual lessons tend to be the profound ones. It's like a key to a mystery of being. In the last year and a half, I've not only said good-bye to three cats whose presence I always treasured, but also broke up with a lover, and watched a dear friend and employer die of cancer. In the process, blessings have come, and with them many childhood wounds have risen to the surface. I welcomed this healing process, but it has made being in human company feel very risky. In contrast, the healing highlighted the pure love, kindness, good nature and generosity of self each cat embodied in their own unique way. I've re-examined how humans relate to each other, with an emotional brutality we've almost come to take for granted, especially from those closest to us. Consciously or unconsciously, we open wounds in each other through our own unhealed pain that gets covered over with an agreed-upon social appearance of being able to take it. Being with Kuthumi this last year, the trees and flowers in my garden, the sky and earth, the spirit of goodness at the heart of all life, has seemed a much richer and safer experience than having to deal with human pretense and denial.

"Waaaaa!" Kuthumi shouts in my heart, healing its wounds, and encourages me to come out again and give the human world another try, using some of the wisdom that worked for him. "Waaaaa!" and picturing him in my mind, I see a way to be whole again, to be loving and genuinely connected with the best in people, through the strength of being independently and joyously centered in the best in myself, as he appeared to be.

For now, my home is empty of cats, and my life is free of attachments. To my surprise, rather than sadness I find an exhilaration in this lightness and freedom that must be what the eastern traditions point to when they speak of nonattachment. Everything feels brand new. No doubt there will be other cats and even other people. Nonattachment doesn't feel like a stopping point but rather a centering from which to re-approach life and relationships in a more balanced way. I feel pulled past emotional habits, like a slate wiped clean, not clinging to the past or mourning. I keep seeing a mental picture of my life, like a newly opened door, while I sniff around it like a cat, cautious and curious. It is a newly opened door of freedom through which light is pouring. Who knows where it leads? Perhaps to a new way of being, those qualities I saw projected in Kuthumi given back to me by him to wear as my own.

Traditionally, a mantra can only be transmitted by one who has already internalized its power. In "Waaaaa!" Kuthumi sang his own love, goodness and joy in being alive, and connected it irresistibly with those sparks, however deeply buried, within everyone he met. "Waaaaa!" I keep hearing in my heart. I don't feel alone.

❁❁❁❁❁❁❁❁

Cassia Berman is a poet, writer and editor who also teaches t'ai chi, qi gong, qi healing, and workshops on women's spirituality. Her poems and articles have appeared in many magazines and anthologies, including *Species Link: The Journal of Interspecies Telepathic Communication.* Her book of poems, *Divine Mother Within Me,* is available from her at 11-1/2 Tannery Brook Road, Woodstock, NY 12498. Some of her very best friends have been cats.

Chapter Eleven

"This tale is the tale of a kitten
Dwelling now with the blessed above,
It vanquished grim Death and High Heaven
For the name of the kitten was Love."
- Leontine Stanfield

The Angel On My Shoulder

By
Kate Solisti

I was just three years old that glorious day in November 1961. The air was crisp and Thanksgiving was just around the corner. My father seemed very excited when he announced that he had a very special surprise for me. We got in the car and drove for what seemed like forever. I tried to beg and wheedle his secret out of him the whole way. We finally pulled up at the house of one of my father's friends. He was a big man, and I was a little afraid of him. But when my father whispered to me, "You'll have to find IT. Look carefully," I forgot about my shyness and began to search the room frantically. Then he said, "Look inside the slipper." I ran to a huge slipper and peeked inside. Two gold eyes peeked back and blinked at me. I gently plucked a beautiful, orange-and-cream colored tabby kitten out of the slipper. I was in love! We named him Dusty.

This was how Dusty came to me. He was my cat, my first "pet," but he was also much, much more. From my very earliest memories, I have been able to hear animals talk. I was talking to trees and birds and animals before I could talk to people. In fact, I don't know if it was because of my special ability, but as a child I felt more at ease in the natural world of animals than in the world of people. I had been longing for a special friend who would understand me and with whom I could talk. Dusty was the answer to my prayers.

We talked about everything! He told me that animals love humans. I asked why nobody else seemed to hear animals. He replied that they had forgotten how, but that someday they would remember. He said I had come into this life to help people remember their connection to animals. I informed him of my parents' concern when I told them what the animals said to me. I said, "They tell me it's just my imagination, that cats and birds don't talk." Dusty advised me to stop telling my parents about my conversations with animals, that it would be easier on everyone. I agreed with a great deal of relief, but some sadness, too. I wished they could understand, but I knew he was right.

The next three years were filled with love and joy and many conversations. Dusty and I were inseparable. He slept with and comforted me when I cried. He attended tea parties and allowed me to dress him in doll clothes and wheel him around in a baby carriage. Grownups who came to the house would notice how patient and tolerant he was with a little girl who did everything to and with him. They would remark, "My God, that cat is just like a dog. He follows her everywhere!" Once, much to my mother's surprise and delight, he even jumped into the bathtub with me. The look on his face was hilarious! I heard him say, "I've gone too far. Cats are not fond of water. I forgot!" He tried to get out with his dignity intact, but couldn't escape my mother's peals of laughter. He allowed her to towel dry him briefly, then ran off to wash himself properly.

When I began kindergarten, I couldn't wait for each day to end so I could go home and tell Dusty about it. He listened attentively. I was like a traveler returning home from my adventures in a faraway land. School was fun, but not where

I truly belonged. I belonged with Dusty and the natural world of my backyard. We walked and talked every day, exploring the creatures, the plants and their relationships. It was heaven!

In September of 1964, I began first grade. Before the first day of school, Dusty sat me down for a very serious talk. He said, "It's time for you to be with people now."

"Why?" I asked. "I don't like people as much as I like animals and plants. Animals and plants love me, but people confuse me!"

"You are a person," he said. "You need to be with people and learn their ways. You chose to be a human in this life, and you'll need human friends."

"Okay," I said. "I'll try."

And I did. I got to know my classmates. I decided I liked reading and phonics. Art and music were lots of fun. I would come home and share my day with my mother. She was very pleased to see me apply myself so well. With all my new interests, Dusty and I began to grow a little apart. He spent less and less time with me, and began staying out at night more often. One night in October, he crawled into bed with me. I hugged him close and he said, "Our work together is finished now. You are doing so well. I am proud of you." I fell asleep remembering his soft words and feeling very good about life.

Kate Solisti works privately with animals and their people as well as teaching and lecturing in the U.S. and Europe. It gives her great joy to help deepen understanding between humans and animals.

Chapter Twelve

"Within your eyes methinks I find
A kind
And thoughtful look of speechless feeling
That mem'ry's loosened cords undid..."
-Frank H. Seldon

Blessings From A Clown

By
Anonymous

When I was a child I used to love to look at the *Britannica Junior Encyclopedia.* Volume D-E had color plates of dogs and I especially loved the picture of the Afghan hound. It had the most beautifully expressive face I'd ever seen on an animal. I wished I could have a dog like that, but I had been told they were very expensive. Since my family was without means, I had no real hope.

During my early teens, I was overtaken by a darkness. By the age of twenty, I had been depressed for several years. Whatever dreams I might have had seemed so unattainable that I avoided dreaming altogether. I felt sad, frustrated, and incapable of deciding to what I should apply myself. After two bewildering years, I dropped out of college to work in a large department store in Harrisburg, Pennsylvania. One day, while I chatted with a co-worker, a woman approached us and asked, "Does anyone want a dog?" Making idle conversation, I asked, "What kind of dog?" She replied, "An Afghan hound." Immediately, I said, "I did", expressing my keen enthusiasm even though I was secretly sure there would be a catch.

But there was no catch. Within the week, I picked up two-year old, Brandy of Alexandria's Cassandra, who had a beautiful blond coat with red saddle, ears blending gradually from blond to red to black, and gorgeous, Cleopatra-like eyes. I could not believe my luck. I loved her instantly.

We left Pennsylvania for New York City. Cassandra and I practically became inseparable. At the time, I was experiencing a seemingly endless bad patch and moved frequently. Whenever I found myself in a situation where a dog would not be tolerated, Cassandra had to be temporarily left with family. It was never for long, but when I eventually retrieved her, she would give lots of attitude and not "talk" to me for days. Finally, I decided I could no longer move to a place where she would not be welcomed. We were in this together. My depression continued and, at times, we lived in abject poverty. Were it not for Cassandra, there were many days that I would not have gotten out of bed at all.

Through it all, Cassandra was my greatest delight. She was a steadfast companion, who consoled me with her presence, and she was genuinely funny. She displayed little of the typical regalness of the Afghan hound in the hilarious positions she managed to assume. She could coil improbably like a snake, as well as sprawl luxuriously on her back or turn completely upside-down in her chair, head on the seat and legs over the arm or up against the back. Viewing our neighborhood from the window, I would offer comments of the goings-on in the street. Cassandra reminded me of a local busybody, leaning on the sill and standing on her hind legs to see if she had missed anything. She looked just like a kid in furry Dr. Dentons. At a time when I had very few laughs, she was there to provide them.

This charming clown was affectionate. She liked to kiss, giving a sharp jab to the lips with her nose, which not everyone appreciated. She had a whole range of vocabulary.

Her assorted barks, with varying levels of intensity, left no doubt as to what she wanted, whether it was cookies, cheese, "her" chair, or to go out. She knew how to get attention, and she knew how to avoid attention when doing something sneaky.

Once I came home to find an entirely empty cracker box lying on the rug in absolutely pristine condition. I couldn't help but laugh as I imagined her opening the closed pantry door, pulling the box down from the third shelf, carrying it to a comfortable spot, working it open, and somehow managing to get every last cracker without damaging the box in any way.

Though the bed was a favorite spot, Cassandra wouldn't think of lying down before she drew the covers from the pillow where she then laid her head. And once, when scolded for lying on my parents' sofa, she proceeded to balance her rump on the cushion, legs dangling over the edge like a person, and looked at me as if to ask, "How about like this?"

Cassandra was with me for 12 years during the very worst times in my life. Through failed relationships, many moves, and terribly disheartening jobs. In all those years, I didn't have a car. I only managed to get her to the Pennsylvania woods a handful of times and that was because our family had a cabin there. We visited the ocean only once, but I often wished I'd had a movie camera for the occasion. There could not have been a more profound expression of pure ecstasy than was on that dog while she ran along the wide, open beach. It was one of the most joyful moments of her entire life.

Slowly, things in my life began to improve. I found work that I could enjoy and I fell in love and married. My husband, Jean-Pierre, loved Cassandra almost as much as I did.

Seven years ago, shortly before Thanksgiving, Cassandra stopped eating. I sat with her for hours each day trying to coax her to take small bits of food. We brought her with us to my parents' home for the holiday. Their yard was deep with snow. In spite of her weakened condition, I took Cassandra outside where she tried to walk further into the woods that bounded my parents' property. She did not want to go back. I understood, but my heart was breaking. I was not ready to let her go. I picked her up and carried her back to the house.

Back in New York in the beginning of December, I knew she was not going to live. Jean-Pierre and I took her to the vet who suggested we put her to sleep. I looked at her and knew I could not end our friendship that way.

We rented a car and took Cassandra to our family's cabin in the Pocono mountains. She managed to walk up the small hill where the cabin sits. Inside, I put blankets on the sofa and made her as comfortable as I could. Cassandra had always been there for me. I felt strongly that she had come into my life to protect me, to prevent my depression from having the last word. While I had thought of leaving this "veil of tears," her very presence necessitated my staying to care for her. Even now, I felt that she was holding on for me. I didn't want her to suffer any more.

I read somewhere that Aldous Huxley had offered his wife encouragement to help her as she died. Now I tried to do the same. As I stroked Cassandra, I kept saying, "It's okay to go now. Just go to the light. I will be all right. It's okay to leave." But evening came, and she was still with us.

Earlier, I had talked with friends of my intention to stay with Cassandra until the end. One friend said, "You know what happens, don't you? When they die, they lose control of their body and it is a horrible mess." I replied that I didn't care. I slept with Cassandra on the sofa. About four in the morning, she got up by herself to use the papers on the floor by the door and, with my help, managed to get back up on the sofa. Again I stroked her, telling her that it was okay to leave now. An hour later, she died. I am convinced that even this last mundane act showed her amazing awareness and considerateness.

I grieved for my friend more than I had for any human, before or since.

Four years ago, I had a psychic reading by a woman I had never met before. She said, "You have a dog spirit that sleeps on your bed at night." I wasn't surprised. Cassandra had always slept on my bed. Imagining her curled or sprawled with her head on my pillow still makes me smile.

The author, who wishes to remain anonymous, is also a painter who lives and works in New York City.

Chapter Thirteen

Saying Good-Bye

*"We who choose to surround ourselves with lives even
more temporary than our own live within a fragile circle,
easily and often breached."*
- Irving Townsend

Throughout history, pets have played an important and supportive role for humanity. Anyone who has loved a pet knows the depth of that relationship is profound and difficult to express. Some people find it easier to develop stronger bonds with an animal than with another human being.

There are several reasons for this. As a psychotherapist, I work with many people who grew up in severely dys-functional homes that were plagued with alcoholism, domestic violence or parental neglect. As a result, these children did not receive the foundation of trust, consistency and safety so essential for healthy development. As they reached adulthood, their relationships often became more troublesome, leaving them feeling isolated and lonely. It is a sad fact that healthy relationships are not possible without a healthy inner relationship of self-esteem and personal self-worth. Thus, pets can serve a very important and healing role by providing an opportunity for nurturance, companionship and a sense of gratification that stems from caring for someone.

Such acceptance and unconditional loyalty often serves as a healing catalyst upon which a new foundation for other relationships can be planted. Love and acceptance can help heal our self-esteem. We can see ourselves through their loving eyes and thereby are elevated in our own. Time and again, I have seen emotionally wounded individuals open up gleefully to a furry companion. A pet is "safe" to love and play with, and does not judge. In the absence of such judgement with its constrictive, oppressive energy, a person can develop a neutral space in which to experience things differently.

Another important factor in the increasing value of the pet relationship has been the breakdown of the traditional family. Susan Phillips Cohen, Director of Counseling at the Animal Medical Center in New York City, states:

> "While people have always become attached to animals that share their environments, recent changes in family structure and mobility have heightened the chances and significance of such attachments. More than ever, Americans live alone or in small groups away from their places of birth, generally in cities or suburbs. In urban environments pets live close to people, providing protection, affection, social opportunities and a chance for one creature to care tenderly for another."

In a rapidly changing world filled with new technology, job restructuring and relocation, often a pet is the only constant relationship. It can serve as an anchor in a world filled with challenges.

It is completely understandable that the loss of a pet can be deeply traumatic. When we lose our closest friend, for instance, we lose a part of our history. Often, grief experienced from the loss of a pet can be as deeply felt and even more profound than the loss of a human being. People need permission to grieve loved ones and get support for this process from friends and family. Sadly, I often meet people who feel ashamed when expressing such emotion to colleagues and friends. The sympathetic response is often minimized, leaving the grief-stricken feeling even more alone and misunderstood. As a result, an increasing number of grief counseling programs are being developed. Many veterinarians and animal health care workers have formed support networks of therapists and other resources to help cope with pet loss.

Herbert A. Nieburg is a psychotherapist specializing in grief therapy and instructs veterinary professionals in the psychological impact of pet death. In his book, *Pet Loss: A Thoughtful Guide For Parents And Children,* he writes:

> "How do we manage to deal with this distress? The sensible answer is that we allow ourselves to mourn - to explore our attachment and admit our sense of loss, to accept the stress and treat it openly. The complication is that we don't want to. We feel embarrassed owning up to our grief over the death of an animal. For our culture, there is really no acceptable way of mourning a pet."

It is my hope that through this publication, we can elevate the pet relationship and its loss to a place of respect and social support. Love is nothing to apologize for, and grief is a demonstration of love.

Letting Go

"Grief is love not wanting to let go."
- Rabbi Earl Grollman

The grieving process that takes place for the death of a human being is the same that is felt for the loss of a beloved pet. In her book, *On Death And Dying,* Elizabeth Kubler-Ross describes four distinct stages. Each stage is normal and should not be treated as a problem to be fixed. The five stages are:

<u>Denial</u>: a defense mechanism used to protect a person from the pain of loss. The person will often behave as if nothing has happened. It hasn't "hit" yet. "Maybe that wasn't Spot hit by the car. Maybe it just looked like him. Maybe he is hiding in the woods and will come home soon."

<u>Anger</u>: It is no wonder that anger would follow the bargaining stage, especially if we feel our prayers went unanswered. Anger can be directed towards the medical profession, or even ourselves if we feel we have somehow failed our loved one. If this anger is turned inward it can result in guilt and self-condemnation. God doesn't care about me. If he did, he wouldn't have let Blacky die. He doesn't care so I don't either."

<u>Bargaining</u>: This is often directed at God before the death. The person promises, pledges and prays to do certain things or behave in a certain way if God will change the course of death for that person or pet. These are often vain attempts to change the will of God. "I"ll never do another bad thing again if you will please just save my cat, Fluffy. She would be so lost without me to protect her."

<u>Acceptance and Resolution</u>: In the fourth and fifth stages of the process, conflict subsides and acceptance takes its place. The person is able to remember without pain and is free to appreciate the gift that was theirs in that special relationship. With resolution may also come the desire for

another pet/companion. "Sparky is in doggy heaven waiting for us, and someday we will all be a big happy family again."

All five stages are a necessary part of letting go of a loved one. It is important to be supported through this process, whenever possible. Support and validation help speed up the healing process and allow the individual to experience loving, caring and sharing. In some cases, however, people need time alone in order to heal without pressure of any kind. Honor this in yourself and in others, but make sure there is balance in this aloneness. If those who grieve are simply isolated and running away from their pain by not talking about it, they may become stuck in the denial phase.

The most important thing to remember if you are grieving is to honor your feelings, surround yourself with understanding people, and give yourself time.

Once we have reached the other side of the process, loving and grieving our loss can leave us with many enriching gifts. I am reminded of Elizabeth Kubler-Ross' words from her book, *Death, The Final Stage Of Growth:*

> "While the experience of the grief work is difficult and slow and wearing, it is also enriching and fulfilling. The most beautiful people we have known are those who have known defeat, known suffering, known struggle, known loss, and have found their way out of the depths. These persons have an appreciation, a sensitivity and an understanding of life that fills them with compassion, gentleness, and a deep loving concern. Beautiful people do not just happen."

I have chosen some of my favorite animal prayers to be used in ceremonies and tributes when you are met with the loss of a beloved pet. I hope you will share these with others who are saying goodbye to a loyal friend.

Animal Prayers

"Good Master, bless each dog and cat that no one owns,
that has no flower bed to bury bones,
no loving hand to scratch his ears,
nor kind words to soothe away the fears,
Yes saints, guard well each cringing kitten and pup,
that slinks with tail turned down instead of up.
Let's pray they will not longer have to roam
because of new found comfort in a loving home."
- Anonymous

♡ ♡ ♡ ♡ ♡

"Blessed are You, Lord God,
for all living creatures You have made.
You keep them in Your care and not one
of them is lost without You knowing.
They glorify You, each in its own way,
and speak to us of Your beauty and Love.
Bless them and keep them from harm.
They unquestionably accept their place in
the rhythm of Your creation.
May we respect them and cherish them
for they are Your gifts to us;
through them may we come to know You
better and praise You, their Creator.
Blessed be the love and joy that they bring to us."
-Amen

♡ ♡ ♡ ♡ ♡

Chinook Blessing Litany

"We call upon the earth, our planet home, with its
beautiful depths and soaring heights, its vitality
and abundance of life, and together we ask that it:
Teach us, and show us the way.

We call upon the mountains, the Cascades and the
Olympics, the high green valleys and meadows
filled with wild flowers, the snows that never melt,
the summits of intense silence, and we ask that
they:
Teach us, and show us the way.

We call upon the waters that rim the earth, horizon to
horizon, that flow in our rivers and streams, that
fall upon our gardens and fields, and we ask that
they:
Teach us, and show us the way.

We call upon the land which grows our food, the
nurturing soil, the fertile fields, the abundant
gardens and orchards, and we ask that they:
Teach us and show us the way.

We call upon the forests, the great trees reaching
strongly to the sky with earth in their roots and the
heavens in their branches, the fir and the pine and
the cedar, and we ask them to:
Teach us, and show us the way.

We call upon the creatures of the fields and forests and
the seas, our brothers and sisters the wolves and
deer, the eagle and dove, the great whales and the
dolphin, the beautiful Orca and salmon who share
our Northwest home, and we ask them to:
Teach us, and show us the way.

We call upon all those who have lived on this earth,
our ancestors and our friends, who dreamed the
best for future generations, and upon whose lives
our lives are built, and with thanksgiving, we call
upon them to:
Teach us, and show us the way.

And lastly, we call upon all that we hold most sacred,
the presence and power of the Great Spirit of love
and truth which flows through all the universe ... to
be with us to:
Teach us, and show us the way."
(from Earth Prayers From Around the World
by Elizabeth Roberts)

♡ ♡ ♡ ♡ ♡

"But ask now the beasts,
and they shall teach thee;
and the fowls of the air,
and they shall tell thee:
Or speak to the earth,
and it shall teach thee:
And the fishes of the sea
shall declare unto thee."
- JOB 12:7-8, KIV

♡ ♡ ♡ ♡ ♡

"Father, in Thy starry tent
I kneel, a humble suppliant...
A dog has died today on earth,
Of little worth
Yet very dear..."
-Dr. Wildred J. Funk

♡ ♡ ♡ ♡ ♡

"O God, scatterer of ignorance and darkness,
grant me your strength.
May all beings regard me with the eye of a friend,
and I all beings!
With the eye of a friend may each single being regard all
others!"
- Sukla Yajur, Veda XXXVI

♡　♡　♡　♡　♡

What About Our Children

"Shared joy is double joy, and shared sorrow is half-sorrow"
- Swedish Proverb

For many children, the loss of a pet is their first experience with the reality of death. When dealing with this delicate subject, the single most important thing for a parent to remember is to be honest. If we try to shelter or protect our children from the pain of loss, we may often make things worse. Pain, grief and loss are all a part of life and if children are supported through their grief process, they will feel stronger and more self-confident

If a pet is sick and clearly close to death, it is helpful to explain the situation and what will probably ensue as a result of this illness. Make sure you tell the child that the illness or old age of the pet is a normal part of life. Some children may blame themselves for their pet's disease. Answer all questions and be careful to explain common terms which can sometimes be misunderstood by a child. Telling a child that you have just put kitty to sleep and she is now in heaven can be very unsettling. The word "sleep" may inadvertently be associated with death and can create undue fear and anxiety in young children. Another taboo is never have an animal euthanized without preparing children beforehand so that they can say their good-byes. Some children may also feel the need to view the body. This is a very individual decision and may be considered the right course for certain children.

Children respond well to ceremonies as part of their process of letting go. They may want to make a paw print of their pet, put together a scrap book or write a poem. Many families prefer to hold a memorial service and invite friends that loved the pet as well to share in their sorrow. This can be an opportunity to read a poem, prayer or letter that you or your child has written to the deceased pet.

"Old friend, your place is empty now. No more
Shall we obey the imperious deep-mouthed call
That begged the instant freedom of our hall."
-Winifred Letts

By honoring our loved ones in their death and paying
tribute to their unique contribution to our lives, we give
ourselves a tremendous gift. We get to say good-bye and
thank you to the one we have loved, as well as demonstrate the
value of life and the importance of living it fully.

One of my favorite prayers and a wonderful tool to live
by is the Serenity Prayer:

God, grant me the Serenity to accept the things I
cannot change,
The Courage to change the things I can,
And the Wisdom to know the difference.

Father, We Thank Thee
"For flowers that bloom about our feet,
Father, we thank thee,
For tender grass so fresh and sweet,
Father, we thank Thee,
For the song of bird and hum of bee,
For all things fair we hear or see,
Father in heaven, we thank Thee.
For blue of stream and blue of sky,
Father, we thank Thee,
For pleasant shade of branches high,
Father, we thank Thee,
For fragrant air and cooling breeze,
For beauty of the blooming trees,
Father in heaven, we thank Thee.
For this new morning with its light
Father, we thank Thee,
For rest and shelter of the night,
Father, we thank Thee,

For health and food, for love and friends,
For everything Thy goodness sends,
Father in heaven, we thank Thee."
- Ralph Waldo Emerson

Tough Decisions

"Every life has a measure of sorrow. Sometimes it is this
that awakens us ."
-Ancient Buddhist Saying

Many pet owners are faced with the tough decision to euthanize their animal. Your veterinarian is certainly the best judge of your animal's physical condition, but you may better understand your pet's emotional condition. Some basic things to look for are: poor appetite, non-responsiveness to the family's attention, lack of interest in their "favorite things", like going for a walk or swim. A pet begins to withdraw from loved ones and sometimes will hide or even go off into the woods. Carole Wilbourn, a well-known cat therapist and author of several books on cat behavior, says in her book, *Cats on the Couch:*

> "Cat's life is dependent on his person's love and support, his own physical strength, his inner will or spirit, and fate. If one of these elements is weak, the others can carry him until the other is refurbished. But if the missing element is vital and cannot be rallied, a cat's end is near.
>
> You can tell when your cat is near the end if he has a faraway, withdrawn look in his eyes, he is nonresponsive to contact, and he hides. If at this time he also appears to be in pain, this is the time to have your vet assist him to the end."

If it seems like the right time to euthanize your pet, there are several decision to make before you begin the procedure. Here are some important questions to ask yourself. Do I want to be with my pet when he/she is euthanized? Many clinics allow the owner and family to be present, but it is important this be thought through and discussed thoroughly. Not everyone can handle watching their pet die. For some people, it can be the final act of love and support for their beloved pet; for others, an additional trauma to an already painful experience. Remember, there is no right or wrong, only a decision that is "right" for you at that time. Many clinics now offer support groups and therapy that specialize in grief counseling. If you feel you need help either with your decision or the aftermath of sorrow, ask your veterinarian for referrals.

Another decision you will need to make is where to bury your pet. If your state allows, you may choose to bury your animal in a favorite spot in the yard. Cremation can be done by the animal control agency in your area, and burial in a pet cemetery.

Wendell Morse, a veterinarian and executive director of the International Association of Pet Cemeteries says: "A very general rule of thumb is that a pet burial costs 10 percent of what it may cost to bury a human." The IAPC's voluntary standards for a good pet cemetery are to have at least five acres of land, an endowed care fund in place, be well maintained, and be restricted by a deed of trust. IAPC can be contacted at: (219) 277-1115.

Perhaps the most beautiful thing I discovered about where to bury your dog appeared in an excerpt from *Old Dogs Remembered* (Carroll & Graf Publishers, Inc. 1993), edited by Bud Johns. This piece by Ben Hur Lampman originally appeared in *The Oregonian*, copyright 1925.

"Yet it is a small matter, and it touches sentiment more than anything else. For if the dog be well remembered, if sometimes he leaps through your dreams actual as in life, eyes kindling, questing, asking, laughing, begging, it matters not at all where that dog sleeps at long and at last. On a hill where the wind is unrebuked, and the trees are roaring, or beside a stream he knew in puppyhood, or somewhere in the flatness of a pasture land, where most exhilarating cattle graze. It is all one to the dog, and all one to you, and nothing is gained, and nothing is lost - if memory lives. But there is one best place to bury a dog. One place that is best of all...The one best place to bury a good dog is in the heart of his master."

May you be as blessed in your grieving as you were in your loving and may all of God's creatures know the comfort of a loving friend.

- Santi

Chapter Fourteen

*"Every single creature is full of God
and is a book about God..."
- By M. Eckhart*

A Year Of Animal Celebrations

*"He Prayeth Well, Who Loveth Well
Both man and bird and beast."
- Samuel Taylor*

*To order a full color art poster of **A YEAR OF ANIMAL
CELEBRATIONS**, call **1-800-335-8553** or e-mail: Galactca
@aol.com or www.GalacticaInst.com.*

January 2000

Sunday	Monday	Tuesday	Wednesday	Thursday	Friday	Saturday
		Dec 1999 S M T W T F S 1 2 3 4 5 6 7 8 9 10 11 12 13 14 15 16 17 18 19 20 21 22 23 24 25 26 27 28 29 30 31	**Feb 2000** S M T W T F S 1 2 3 4 5 6 7 8 9 10 11 12 13 14 15 16 17 18 19 20 21 22 23 24 25 26 27 28 29			*1* New Year's Day - Celebration of life
2	*3* Death of Joy Adamson in Kenya, 1980 - Author of "Born Free"	*4*	*5*	*6*	*7*	*8*
9	*10*	*11*	*12*	*13*	*14* Birthday of Albert Schweitzer - Humanitarian and friend of all animals	*15*
16	*17* Gray whale migration in North America	*18*	*19*	*20*	*21*	*22*
23	*24*	*25*	*26*	*27*	*28*	*29*
30	*31*					

February 2000

Sunday	Monday	Tuesday	Wednesday	Thursday	Friday	Saturday
		1	2	3	4	5
6	7	8	9	10	11	12 Festival of Diana (Artemis) - Protector of wildlife and forest
13	14	15	16	17	18	19
20	21	22	23	24	25	26
27	28	29				

Jan 2000

S	M	T	W	T	F	S
						1
2	3	4	5	6	7	8
9	10	11	12	13	14	15
16	17	18	19	20	21	22
23	24	25	26	27	28	29
30	31					

Mar 2000

S	M	T	W	T	F	S
			1	2	3	4
5	6	7	8	9	10	11
12	13	14	15	16	17	18
19	20	21	22	23	24	25
26	27	28	29	30	31	

March 2000

Sunday	Monday	Tuesday	Wednesday	Thursday	Friday	Saturday
Feb 2000 / Apr 2000			1	2	3	4
5	6	7	8	9	10	11
12 Crane Watch Day	13	14	15	16	17	18
19 National Agriculture Day - Swallows return to San Juan Capistrano	20	21	22	23	24	25
26	27	28	29	30	31	

Feb 2000

S	M	T	W	T	F	S
		1	2	3	4	5
6	7	8	9	10	11	12
13	14	15	16	17	18	19
20	21	22	23	24	25	26
27	28	29				

Apr 2000

S	M	T	W	T	F	S
						1
2	3	4	5	6	7	8
9	10	11	12	13	14	15
16	17	18	19	20	21	22
23	24	25	26	27	28	29
30						

April 2000

Sunday	Monday	Tuesday	Wednesday	Thursday	Friday	Saturday
		Mar 2000 S M T W T F S 1 2 3 4 5 6 7 8 9 10 11 12 13 14 15 16 17 18 19 20 21 22 23 24 25 26 27 28 29 30 31	**May 2000** S M T W T F S 1 2 3 4 5 6 7 8 9 10 11 12 13 14 15 16 17 18 19 20 21 22 23 24 25 26 27 28 29 30 31			1
2	3	4	5	6	7	8
9	10	11	12	13	14 National Dolphin Day - Remembrance of all sea creatures	15
16	17	18	19	20	21	22
23 Easter - First Sunday after full moon, Rebirth of Nature	24	25	26	27	28	29
30						

May 2000

Sunday	Monday	Tuesday	Wednesday	Thursday	Friday	Saturday
	1 Be Kind to Animals' Week	2	3	4	5	6 Shepherds' and Hersdman's Day (Eastern Europe)
7	8	9	10	11	12	13
14	15	16	17	18	19	20
21 National Dog Bite Prevention Week	22	23	24	25	26	27
28	29	30	31			

Apr 2000

S	M	T	W	T	F	S
						1
2	3	4	5	6	7	8
9	10	11	12	13	14	15
16	17	18	19	20	21	22
23	24	25	26	27	28	29
30						

Jun 2000

S	M	T	W	T	F	S
				1	2	3
4	5	6	7	8	9	10
11	12	13	14	15	16	17
18	19	20	21	22	23	24
25	26	27	28	29	30	

June 2000

Sunday	Monday	Tuesday	Wednesday	Thursday	Friday	Saturday
	May 2000 / Jul 2000			1	2 Seamen's Day (Iceland)	3
4	5	6	7	8	9	10
11	12	13	14	15	16	17
18	19	20	21	22	23	24
25	26	27	28	29	30	

May 2000

S	M	T	W	T	F	S
	1	2	3	4	5	6
7	8	9	10	11	12	13
14	15	16	17	18	19	20
21	22	23	24	25	26	27
28	29	30	31			

Jul 2000

S	M	T	W	T	F	S
						1
2	3	4	5	6	7	8
9	10	11	12	13	14	15
16	17	18	19	20	21	22
23	24	25	26	27	28	29
30	31					

July 2000

Sunday	Monday	Tuesday	Wednesday	Thursday	Friday	Saturday
		Jun 2000 S M T W T F S 1 2 3 4 5 6 7 8 9 10 11 12 13 14 15 16 17 18 19 20 21 22 23 24 25 26 27 28 29 30	**Aug 2000** S M T W T F S 1 2 3 4 5 6 7 8 9 10 11 12 13 14 15 16 17 18 19 20 21 22 23 24 25 26 27 28 29 30 31			1
2	3	4 Independenc Day (U.S.) - Freedom for all living beings	5	6	7	8
9	10	11	12	13	14 Bastille Day (France) - A day of liberation	15 Obon - Japanese Lantern Festival
16	17	18	19	20	21	22
23	24	25	26	27	28	29
30	31					

August 2000

Sunday	Monday	Tuesday	Wednesday	Thursday	Friday	Saturday
Jul 2000 S M T W T F S 1 2 3 4 5 6 7 8 9 10 11 12 13 14 15 16 17 18 19 20 21 22 23 24 25 26 27 28 29 30 31		1 Hopi Snake Dance Festival - Praying to Great Spirit for rain	2	3	4	5
6	7	8	9	10	11	12
13	14	15	16	17	18	19
20	21	22	23	24	25	26
27	28	29	30	31	**Sep 2000** S M T W T F S 1 2 3 4 5 6 7 8 9 10 11 12 13 14 15 16 17 18 19 20 21 22 23 24 25 26 27 28 29 30	

September 2000

Sunday	Monday	Tuesday	Wednesday	Thursday	Friday	Saturday
	Aug 2000 S M T W T F S 1 2 3 4 5 6 7 8 9 10 11 12 13 14 15 16 17 18 19 20 21 22 23 24 25 26 27 28 29 30 31	Oct 2000 S M T W T F S 1 2 3 4 5 6 7 8 9 10 11 12 13 14 15 16 17 18 19 20 21 22 23 24 25 26 27 28 29 30 31			*1* Jewish Month of Ellul - Time of renewal and reconciliation with the natural world	*2*
3	*4*	*5*	*6*	*7*	*8*	*9*
10	*11*	*12*	*13*	*14*	*15* Feast of Holy Cross and Feast of Our Lady of Sorrows - Prayerful day to mourn extinction of species	*16*
17 National Farm Animals' Awareness Week	*18*	*19*	*20*	*21*	*22*	*23* Worldwide Day of Prayer and Meditation to Help Heal Mother Earth
24	*25*	*26*	*27*	*28*	*29*	*30*

October 2000

Sunday	Monday	Tuesday	Wednesday	Thursday	Friday	Saturday
1	2	3	4 Feast of St. Francis of Assisi - Patron saint of the animals	5	6	7
8 Columbus Day - Celebrate Native American teachings about the earth	9	10	11	12	13	14
15	16	17	18	19	20	21
22	23 The swallows leave San Juan Capistrano Mission	24	25	26	27	28
29	30	31				

Sep 2000

S	M	T	W	T	F	S
					1	2
3	4	5	6	7	8	9
10	11	12	13	14	15	16
17	18	19	20	21	22	23
24	25	26	27	28	29	30

Nov 2000

S	M	T	W	T	F	S
			1	2	3	4
5	6	7	8	9	10	11
12	13	14	15	16	17	18
19	20	21	22	23	24	25
26	27	28	29	30		

November 2000

Sunday	Monday	Tuesday	Wednesday	Thursday	Friday	Saturday
Oct 2000 S M T W T F S 1 2 3 4 5 6 7 8 9 10 11 12 13 14 15 16 17 18 19 20 21 22 23 24 25 26 27 28 29 30 31	Dec 2000 S M T W T F S 1 2 3 4 5 6 7 8 9 10 11 12 13 14 15 16 17 18 19 20 21 22 23 24 25 26 27 28 29 30 31	**1** All Saints' Day - For all the creatures that give their lives so that we may live	**2** All Souls' Day - Feast of the Dead	**3**	**4**	
5	**6**	**7**	**8**	**9**	**10**	**11**
12	**13**	**14**	**15**	**16**	**17**	**18**
19	**20**	**21**	**22**	**23** Thanksgiving Day - Fourth Thursday of month, to celebrate the abundance and nourishment of the earth	**24**	**25**
26	**27**	**28**	**29**	**30**		

December 2000

Sunday	Monday	Tuesday	Wednesday	Thursday	Friday	Saturday
	Nov 2000 S M T W T F S / 1 2 3 4 / 5 6 7 8 9 10 11 / 12 13 14 15 16 17 18 / 19 20 21 22 23 24 25 / 26 27 28 29 30 **Jan 2001** S M T W T F S / 1 2 3 4 5 6 / 7 8 9 10 11 12 13 / 14 15 16 17 18 19 20 / 21 22 23 24 25 26 27 / 28 29 30 31				1	2
3	4	5	6	7 Feast of St. Ambrose - Patron Saint of domestic animals	8	9
10	11	12	13	14	15	16
17	18	19	20	21	22	23
24	25 Christmas Day - Birthday of Jesus	26	27	28	29	30
31						

Notes

Page 4   (1)Elwyn Hartley Edwards. *All About Horses.* New York: Dorling Kindersley, Inc., 1991.

Page 4   (2)Roger A. Caras. *A Celebration of Cats.* New York: Simon & Schuster, 1986.

Pages 4 (3)(4)Don Harper. *Dogs.* New Jersey: Chartwell
&5   Books, Inc., 1994 pp. 15, 16, 23, 24, 27, 28.

Page 7   (5)Jeffrey Moussaieff Masson and Susan McCarthy. *When Elephants Weep, The Emotional Lives of Animals.* New York: Delacourt Press, 1995 p. 160.

Page 7   (6)Nancy Plevin. *The New Mexican,* Health & Science Section, February 9, 1996, C1 & 2.

Pages 8 (7)(8)Liz Palika. "Therapy and Service Dogs, Cold
& 9   Noses and Warm Hearts." *Newsweek Magazine,* Special Section: All About Pets. For free reprints, write to:
         Mark J. Saferstein
         Creative Manager, Special Opportunities
         Newsweek Magazine
         P.O. Box 3001
         Livingston, NJ 07039-7001
         Attention: All About Pets Reprints

Page 12 (9)*N.W. American Health Magazine*, September 1996, p.46.

Page 17 (10)Rupert Sheldrake, "The Case of the Telepathic Pet." *New Age Journal*, September/October, 1995.

References

Anderson, Moira. "Coping With Sorrow," *Dog Fancy Magazine* (September, 1986) p.46-51.

Isler, Wendy. "A Time To Mourn," *Advocate* (Winter, 1987) p.9-10.

Gonzalez, Philip and Leonore Fleischer. *The Dog Who Rescues Cats, The True Story of Jinny.* New York: HarperCollins Publishers, 1995.

Harper, Don. *Dogs.* New Jersey: Chartwell Books, Inc., 1994.

Johns, Bud. *Old Dogs Remembered.* Carroll & Graf Publishers, 1993.

Klein, Marty. *Blind Sighted, One Man's Journey From Sight To Insight.* New York: Baba Doofus Publishing Company, 1993.

Kubler-Ross, Elizabeth. *Death, The Final Stage of Growth.* New Jersey: Prentice-Hall, Inc., 1975.

Kubler-Ross, Elizabeth. On Death and Dying. New York: MacMillian Publishing.

Mortenson, Joseph. *Whale Songs and Wasps Maps, The Mystery of Animal Thinking.* New York: E.P. Dutton, 1987.

Masson, Moussaieff Jeffrey and Susan McCarthy. *When Elephants Weep, The Emotional Lives of Animals.* New York: Delacort Press, 1995.

Neiburg, Herbert A. and Arlene Fischer. *Pet Loss: A Thoughtful Guide for Adults and Children.* New York: Harper & Row, 1982.

Schoen, D.V.M., Allen M. and Pam Proctor. *Love, Miracles, and Animal Healing.* New York: Simon & Schuster, 1995.

Seibert, Dianan, Judy C. Drolet and Joyce V. Fetro. *Are You Sad Too? Helping Children Deal With Loss and Death.* California: ETR Associates, 1993.

Sheldrake, Rupert. *Seven Experiments That Could Change The World.* Riverhead Books.

Stapen, Canyce H. "When Your Pet Dies," *Better Homes & Gardens.* (Nov./Dec. 1994), p.31-33.

Wilbourn, Carole C. *Cats On The Couch, The Complete Guide For Loving And Caring For Your Cat.* New York: The Humane Society of New York, 1988.

Wilhelm, Hans. *I'll Always Love You.* Dragonfly Books.

Animal Organizations & Training Centers

American Animal Hospital Association (AAHA). For brochure on more than 13,000 veterinarians committed to excellence, send a self-addressed stamped envelope to: AAHA Pet Care Exams, P.O. Box 150899, Denver, CO 80215-0899. (800) 252-2242.

Animals As Intermediaries (AAI) c/o Seabury School, Inc. P.O. Box 155, Concord, MA 01742. (978) 369-2585. Educational and therapeutic programs that bring the world of nature into closed-care institutions.

Animal Telepathy Experiment. Write to: *New Age Journal*, 42 Pleasant Street, Watertown, MA 02472. (617) 926-0200

Canine Companions-New Mexico Champions, 208 Hyde Park Estates, Santa Fe, NM 87501 or call Susan Bloch: (505) 983-3650. Anyone interested in becoming a puppy raiser or applying for a dog companion. These dogs are trained to work with children and adults with special needs.

The Delta Society, 289 Perimeter Road East, Renton, WA 98055. Therapy and Service Dogs. (425) 226-7357

Dogs For The Deaf, Inc., 10175 Wheeler Road, Central Point, OR 97502 voice/TDD (541) 826-9220.

Equine Muscle Therapy & Rehabilitation. (Kate Kennedy Eq.T.P.M.) P.O. Box 72, Colebrook, CT 06021. (860) 379-3863.

Let's Talk, Telepathic Animal Communication. P.O. Box 0621, Colebrook, CT 06021.

Love On A Leash, 3809 Plaza Drive #107-309, Oceanside, CA 92056. Therapy and service dogs.

Kate Solisti, Animal Communication, P.O. Box 841, Conifer, CO 80433. (303) 838-7698.

About The Author

Pamela Santi Meunier is a psychotherapist, lecturer, writer and artist.

In 1990, she co-founded, with her husband, Galactica Institute for Human Development in Western Massachusetts, dedicated to the pursuit of personal and professional excellence.

In addition to holding a Master's Degree in Counseling Psychology from Norwich University, she is also a certified hypnotherapist and yoga therapist. Her work is holistic in nature and explores the full spectrum of the human experience. With her husband and co-worker, Christopher Curren, she teaches a 90-Day Success and Empowerment Program for professionals and individuals from all walks of life. Her unique style of teaching has been credited with creating a turning point for countless lives, careers and marriages.

Ms. Meunier is a life-long animal lover and nature enthusiast and has dedicated this book to her golden retriever, Tosha, whose story is found in Chapter Two.

Order Form

Galactica Press
25 Hamilton Ave,
Jamestown, RI 02835
800-335-8553
galactca@aol.com   www.galacticainst.com

Name _____

Street Address _____

City _____

State _____ Zip/Postal Code _____

Country _____ E-Mail _____

Product Name	Unit Price	Total
The Obsidian Trials, ppbk	$14.95 @	
Angels With Fur, Ppbk	$16.95 @	
AudioTape: Healing Your Inner Child	$ 8.95 @	
Sales Tax (RI residents only)	7%	
Shipping & Handling	$3.50 per order	
		Total

Method of Payment: ___Check ___Visa ___ MasterCard
Credit Card # _____ Exp. Date _____

Signature _____